MW00785124

Practical Life Skills for Teens

Your Guide To Becoming A Capable, Confident and Independent Teenager With Real-World Skills Not Taught In School - Manage Money, Cook, Self-Care & Many More!

Ben Clardy

❀ Created with Vellum

Mind = Blown

I'm proud of what you did.

The way you picked up this book — opened it — and began reading.

Very impressive!

You just wouldn't believe the number of people who *want* great things in life but aren't able to take even the first tiny step.

Not you, though... *you're different,* and you're already proving it.

Your timing really couldn't be better, either.

You're at the PERFECT age to learn a handful of absolutely critical skills that will practically guarantee a phenomenal future for yourself.

To guide you, I create this series of three amazing books.

 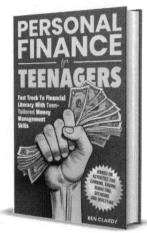 

📙 **_Practical Life Skills For Teens:_** _(This book)_ It's your guide to mastering all the essential abilities that school doesn't teach. It'll help you be a more confident, capable, and well-rounded person so you'll be better prepared for life's inevitable challenges. It's going to be an amazing ride, and I'm excited to get started!

📙 **_Personal Finance For Teens:_** This one is your blueprint for learning different ways to make money, save, budget, and start building financial independence. This stuff is so very important — and it's actually a whole lot of fun, _I promise._

📙 **_Growth Mindset For Teens:_** When you're ready to become an unstoppable, goal-crushing, dream-building machine — this book has got your back. You'll learn the same techniques that athletes, innovators, and high-achievers use to transform setbacks into stepping stones. Very _HIGHLY_ recommended.

* * *

Think of these three books as your personal success toolkit.

While each book stands powerfully on its own, together they form something truly extraordinary — _a complete system for teenage success._

For now, though, let's focus on the transformative journey ahead in these pages.

A future of limitless potential awaits...

Contents

Introduction

Some people want it to happen, some wish it would happen,
and others make it happen. —Michael Jordan

Picture this: You're on the verge of adulthood, ready to take on the world, armed with a boatload of knowledge from school, but suddenly, you're hit with a jarring realization...

You have some "book smarts", but you're also woefully lacking the basic skills needed to survive day-to-day life once you're on your own. I'm talking about the *practical stuff*—like cooking a meal without setting off the smoke alarm, managing your money without ending up with a piggy bank full of IOUs, changing a flat tire without calling for reinforcements, or even ironing a shirt without turning it into origami.

Don't worry—you're not alone in this... *not by a long shot.*

In fact, a study revealed that more than 60% of parents express concern about their teenage children's lack **of practical life skills**. (Elsworthy, 2019).

It's a mind-blowing statistic that raises the question:

If "life skills" are so important, why aren't they teaching us this stuff in school?

That, my friend, is a question that echoes through countless households, leaving teens feeling like they're in a game where everyone knows the rules except them—*but fear not*—because that's precisely where this book comes to the rescue.

Introduction

This book was designed with *you* in mind. It's a fun, engaging, and downright teen-friendly approach that makes learning life skills feel like a breeze. No more snooze-fest lectures or 2-inch-thick textbooks. Instead, we're diving into the nitty-gritty with a sense of humor and relatability.

I get it. Being a teen is like juggling kittens while riding a unicycle on a tightrope. It's challenging, confusing as heck, and sometimes makes you want to scream into a pillow, but it can also be a wild and hilarious adventure! That's why every page is tailored to you, your crazy big dreams, your unique challenges, and your epic journey into adulthood.

But here's the deal—*this book isn't a spectator sport*. I want you to be an active player in this game. Take it chapter by chapter, try the activities, and put those new skills to the test. To develop, grow, and progress, you have to roll up your sleeves and make things happen.

To get the most from this book, grab a journal and jot down your thoughts, track your progress, and take notes of the *lightbulb moments* you encounter throughout this book. You see, growing is not about perfection; *it's about progress*. By taking notes along the way, you'll be able to look back and *actually see* your progress in a tangible, measurable way—and that's an encouraging thing!

So, are you ready to get started? I hope so because this is *your journey*, and it's going to be nothing short of amazing.

Let's do this.

Chapter 1

Thinking Skills

You are today where your thoughts have brought you; you will be tomorrow where your thoughts take you.
—James Allen

To kick things off, let's focus on the most critical area of all—the 6" or so between your ears. That'd be your brain or, more specifically, *your mind*.

Ever feel like your thoughts are running wild and in all directions like a pack of energetic puppies? Don't worry; we've all been there. In this chapter, we'll explore the power of your thoughts, how they shape your reality, and most importantly, how to harness them to bend reality to your will.

Critical Thinking

Anyone with a skull full of grey matter can think, but those who are able to think in a manner that is independent, clear, and rational are *critical thinkers*. Anybody can do it, but it takes practice. The trouble is that people are generally told what to think throughout their lives and, therefore, never develop the skill of thinking *critically* for themselves. Not you, though... you're different!

Picture critical thinking as connecting the dots in your mind—forming your opinions, diving into analysis, and ultimately reaching an intelligent conclusion. To get there, you ask questions beyond the usual "yes or no" variety. Instead, you must dive into the "whys" and "hows."

Example:

Imagine scrolling through your feed and stumbling upon a viral post about a new study claiming that drinking seven cups of coffee daily will make you a genius. It sounds incredible, right? You feel a little jittery just thinking about it. But hold up —let's engage the brain and think about this *critically*...

First, question the source. Is this post from a credible health news outlet or a random meme page? Look for the study itself. Find the original source of information rather than relying on second-hand news, which almost inevitably tends to twist and obscure the facts.

Next, dive into the context. Does the article explain who conducted the study and who funded it? Knowing who's behind the info can reveal a lot about why it was presented in a certain way. *Was it a coffee company* that made the claim? Hmm, the plot thickens!

Now, analyze the claims. Seven cups of coffee a day sounds a bit much, doesn't it? (twitch, twitch) Check out what other experts are saying. A quick search might show you that most health experts recommend moderation. See, those claims are already looking a bit shaky.

Finally, think about the implications. Sharing misleading health advice can be harmful. It's not just about not spreading fake news; it's about being a responsible online community member.

By questioning the source, understanding the context, analyzing the claims, and considering the consequences, you've just navigated the maze of misinformation like a true critical thinker.

So, next time you come across a sensational claim, remember to put your cerebral supercomputer to work. Who knows? You might save your friends from believing they can drink their way to Einstein status, one cup of coffee after another and another and another and...

Creative Thinking

Let's dive into the exciting world of creative thinking, where the sky's the limit and your imagination knows no bounds. Being a creative thinker isn't just about coming up with cool ideas; it's about exploring new horizons, solving problems innovatively, and embracing the unique quirks that make you—well, you!

So, how do you unleash your inner creative genius? The good news is that there are endless possibilities waiting for you to explore.

Let's break it down:

Think Outside The Box: Choose a random word or object—it could be anything from "banana" to "umbrella" to "spaceship." Now, brainstorm ways that this word could be related to your problem or task at hand. At first, this might seem like a stretch—after all, what does a banana have to do with solving a problem or planning a birthday party? But that's precisely the point. By forcing yourself to make connections between seemingly unrelated concepts, you're training your brain to think outside the box. Maybe the shape of a banana inspires a new approach to solving a complex problem, or perhaps the vibrant colors of an umbrella spark ideas for a creative art project.

Try Reverse Thinking: Instead of approaching a problem in the usual way, try flipping it on its head. Begin by envisioning the end goal and then trace back the necessary steps to reach it. This approach can uncover unconventional solutions that may not have been considered otherwise.

Set A Timer: By artificially limiting how much time you have to think, you might force a brilliant idea to the surface as your mind races to find a solution. 60 seconds or so should do it. Extra points if you use a ticking timer for added artificial stress. It kinda feels like a bomb scene from an action movie. *tick *tick *tick *tick... Sounds a bit out there, I know, but it works! Just don't flip your lid when the buzzer goes off.

Daydream: Our most creative ideas often emerge when relaxed and not actively focused on a task. Take breaks from screens and distractions to allow your mind to wander freely. Sometimes, the best solutions come when you're not trying so hard to find them.

As you can see, there are countless ways to embrace creative thinking. So, explore, experiment, and let your imagination run wild.

Making Good Choices

Life is a series of choices—big, small, and those that make you pause and wonder. Making good decisions is like being the captain of your own ship; you steer, navigate, and sometimes brave stormy seas. But what if I told you that you have the power to *make firm and good decisions* that set the course for your life's journey?

Life is like a choose-your-own-adventure book and each decision you make shapes the plot. Each little choice you make, whether big or small, ultimately contributes to your life's path in one way or another. The clothes you wear, whether you keep a clean or messy room, and the friends you choose—all impact your life's outcome. *The choices you make are the building blocks of your future*. This is why developing the habit of making good choices is essential.

The trickiest part about making good choices is that they can often be the most difficult. For instance, doesn't it sound nice to play video games, eat junk food, and skip cleaning your room? Sure, it does, but doing those things regularly will impact your life in negative ways. If you did those things long term, you'd be out of shape, unorganized, develop poor eyesight, and may not have much of a social life. Build the habit of making tough but good decisions, and you're doing your future self a HUGE favor.

Now, let's talk about how emotions affect our decision-making. Have you ever made a choice based on how you felt in the moment, only to regret it later? I know I sure have. We've all been there. Emotions can steer your decisions in odd directions—sometimes helpful, sometimes way off course. But fear not; understanding your emotions is like having a GPS for your feelings. It's about knowing why you feel the way you do and how to navigate those emotions to steer your ship in the right direction, even in the midst of life's emotional storms.

Here's something else that can help your decision-making skills...

Let me introduce you to BRAIN & GUT—the dynamic decision-making duo. Some choices are as clear as a sunny day, like knowing that 2 + 2 equals 4. That's your brain talking. But then there are those moments when your gut nudges you in a direction that logic can't quite explain. It's like having two guides—one armed with facts and figures (brain), the other with instinct and intuition (gut).

So, when should you listen to your brain, and when should you trust your gut? In those situations, you must balance rational thinking and intuitive nudges. When you weigh the feedback you get from your brain and gut, you're navigating the thin line between certainty and uncertainty. The right answer, more often than not, is found somewhere between the two.

Problem-Solving Strategies

Whether choosing between two birthday parties or figuring out how to share the Xbox without a family feud, problem-solving is a skill you need. You don't have to know all the answers; you need a strategy, a game plan for when life throws a curveball your way.

Have you ever faced a problem that seemed so complex that you felt there was no solution? Your first instinct might be to run for the hills. But wait—don't hit the panic button just yet. Breaking down big problems into bite-sized pieces is an excellent way of simplifying the complex.

Here's a simple example:

Bedroom Disaster Remediation

Your bedroom *was* a disaster waiting to happen, but then it *actually happened*. Not all at once, but gradually over days and weeks—almost so slowly that you didn't even see the mess until it was too late. Currently, where there used to be open floor space, there is now a vast assortment of clothes, belongings, magazines, and—*is that a half-eaten sandwich??* There are narrow foot-trails of bare floor connecting the door to the bed to the dresser to the closet to the... *seriously, who leaves a half-eaten sandwich lying around?* At this point, your bedroom seems too overwhelming even to start cleaning, but it must be done. Here's how to get it done by simplifying the problem.

Breaking Down The BIG Problem

Divide the room into distinct areas: closet, desk, bed, and shelves.

Tackle One Section at a Time

- **Closet**: Start by sorting clothes. Make piles to keep, donate, and throw away. Organize the kept clothes by type and color.
- **Desk**: Clear off all papers and supplies. Sort papers into keep, recycle, or shred. Organize school supplies into drawers or organizers.
- **Bed**: Make the bed and arrange pillows. This instantly improves the overall look and makes it feel more manageable.
- **Shelves**: Remove everything from the shelves, dust them, and then return only the items you need or love.
- **Set Time Limits**: Dedicate a specific amount of time to each section, say 30 minutes. This prevents fatigue and keeps the task manageable.
- **Take Breaks**: Take a 5-10 minute break after each section. This helps to refresh and maintain motivation.
- **Outcome**: By addressing each section individually, what seemed like an insurmountable task became completely achievable. Within a couple of hours, the bedroom was organized, and the initial overwhelming feeling was replaced with a sense of accomplishment.

A Simple Problem-Solving Sequence

Let me share a neat little playbook for effective problem-solving. These six steps are your roadmap when you are stuck with a problem that seems insurmountable:

- First things first—what's the problem? It's like creating a treasure map; you must know where "X" marks the spot.
- Let's dive deeper. Why does this matter to you? What's at the heart of the issue? Understanding the *why* will give you direction.
- Get those creative juices flowing. List all the ways you could tackle the problem. Consider them all without judgment. Everything from sensible to a bit out there.
- It's time to play judge and jury. Look at the pros and cons of each solution. Cross off the ones that don't cut it, and rate the rest. We're getting closer to the winning solution.
- You've picked your champion solution. Now, how will it work in the real world? Plan it out.
- Once you've implemented the plan, check how it went. What worked well? What didn't?

Now go out there, face those challenges, and remember, not all problems are roadblocks; some are just detours to a better solution.

Developing a Growth Mindset

Having what's known as a *growth mindset* can make all the difference in facing many of life's challenges. Think of a growth mindset as your secret weapon against self-doubt and fear. Your success hinges on the belief that dedication and hard work can cultivate your abilities rather than viewing them as innate, unchangeable traits from birth. *That's a sentence worth reading again.* In other words, it's the belief that you can conquer any mountain, slay any dragon, and achieve your wildest dreams with belief, effort, and perseverance.

Having a growth mindset means believing—truly believing—that you can achieve anything you put your mind to and commit to the process of making it happen.

Let me tell you something that may be hard to believe but is one of the most genuine things I can say to you:

You're capable of far, FAR more than you think you are.

When you believe this too, the sky is the limit for your accomplishments. Do yourself a big favor. Believe in yourself.

Embracing a growth mindset can level up your thinking skills. Imagine your brain as a muscle. The more you exercise it, the stronger it becomes. Adopting a growth mindset allows you to flex your mental muscles and expand your capacity for creativity, problem-solving, decision-making, and dream-achieving.

Instead of seeing challenges as roadblocks, you view them as opportunities for growth and learning. Did you fail a math test? No problem—it's not a reflection of your intelligence but a chance to learn from your mistakes and improve. Adopting a growth mindset when facing challenges unleashes your complete potential. It enables you to confront even the most challenging endeavors with assurance.

But the journey doesn't end there. Developing a growth mindset isn't just about facing challenges head-on. It's also about embracing the power of reflection and continuous learning. Picture this: after slaying a particularly challenging dragon, you take a moment to reflect on your battle strategies. What worked well? What could you have done differently?

By analyzing your experiences and learning from successes and failures, you're sharpening your thinking skills and laying the groundwork for future victories. Remember, the quest for knowledge is never-ending, and each new lesson learned is a stepping stone toward becoming the ultimate hero of your own story.

Wrap-Up

Remember that sentence that I said was worth reading again?

Well, here it is again:

Your success hinges on the belief that dedication and hard work can cultivate your abilities rather than viewing them as innate, unchangeable traits from birth.

It's important because not only is it true, but it also flies in the face of one of society's most damaging lies—the lie that your fate is predetermined by birth, race, location, status, etc.

The only thing stopping you from being or accomplishing anything you want is— you. Therefore, if you believe that you can achieve it and dedicate yourself to the process of making it happen, then your success is inevitable... it's only a matter of time.

With belief, effort, and perseverance, you can conquer any mountain, slay any dragon, and achieve your wildest dreams.

ACTIVITY: Pros and Cons List

Think of a decision you're currently facing, whether choosing between two extracurricular activities, deciding on a weekend outing, or figuring out how to manage your time effectively.

Grab a pen and paper or open a note-taking app on your device. Create two columns: "Pros" and "Cons." Then, start brainstorming! List all the potential benefits or positive aspects of each option in the "Pros" column and all the drawbacks or negative elements in the "Cons" column. Be honest and thorough in your evaluation.

Once you've listed everything that comes to mind, take a step back and review your lists. This simple exercise can help you gain clarity, weigh your options more objectively, and make informed decisions that align with your aspirations.

Chapter 2
Communication Skills

Effective communication starts with listening.
—Catherine Pulsifer

Ever heard the saying, "It's not just what you say, but how you say it"? Well, get ready to step into the art of effective communication, where listening is just as important as speaking, if not MORE important. In this chapter, we'll explore the power of words, the magic of body language, and the importance of active listening.

Listening vs. Hearing

Hearing is like being at a party while someone is talking to you, but instead of being engaged in the conversation, you're half-heartedly bobbing your head to the music while eyeing the snack table. You might catch a few words here and there, but your brain is on vacation in a mythical place some refer to as "la-la-land," dreaming of the delectable treats that await you.

But listening? That's where the real magic happens! You're not just hearing their words; you're absorbing them like a sponge, trying to understand their thoughts, feelings, and experiences. When you truly listen, you're showing the other person that they matter, that their words have value. It's almost like *feeling the words* that another person is saying.

So, the next time someone starts talking to you, put down your phone, forget about that hilarious meme you saw earlier, stop eyeing the snack table, and give them your undivided attention. Trust me, it's a skill that will make you stand out in a world full of distracted zombies.

Active Listening

Picture this: you're chatting with a friend about their latest adventure, but instead of just nodding along, you're fully engaged in the conversation. You're making eye contact, nodding at the right moments, and maybe even throwing in a "Wow, that sounds amazing!" or two. That, my friend, is active listening in action!

Active listening is like giving someone the VIP treatment during a conversation. It's about showing genuine interest in what they're saying, asking follow-up questions, and really understanding their perspective.

Put your active listening skills to the test. Trust me, the folks you're conversing with will appreciate it, and your conversations will be ten times more meaningful. You'll be amazed at how much deeper your connections can become when you hear what the other person is saying AND the other person KNOWS they're being heard. It's a powerful combination.

Open-Ended Questions

Another element of truly effective communication is asking good questions. You see, asking questions isn't just about getting answers; it's about showing curiosity and opening up new avenues of conversation.

Think about it like this: If you ask someone a closed-ended question like "Did you have a good day?" you'll probably get a simple "yes" or "no" response, but if you ask an open-ended question like "What was the best part of your day?" you're inviting them to share more details and insights. So, try peppering your conversation with open-ended questions. It will keep the conversation flowing, and you'll learn much more about the people around you.

Remember, verbal communication is about building connections and understanding others, whether you're actively listening or asking questions. So, sharpen those listening skills and get in the habit of asking some thought-provoking questions!

Starting the Conversation

Ah, the age-old dilemma of starting a conversation without feeling like a deer in headlights! It can feel like being handed a microphone and told to entertain a crowd of strangers. But fear not, my friend, for I have a secret weapon: *open-ended questions*!

Instead of the classic "Hi, how are you?", try something like, "What's the coolest thing you've done lately? This not only shows that you're genuinely interested in getting to know the other person but also opens the door to a world of fascinating stories.

Another surefire way to get the conversation flowing is to find common ground. Maybe you both have a deep, unwavering love for a particular band or perhaps you've both recently discovered the joys of cooking. Sharing these common interests is like finding a secret handshake.

So, the next time you find yourself in a social situation, remember: open-ended questions and common ground are your trusty sidekicks. With these conversational tools at your disposal, you'll be navigating the treacherous waters of small talk like a seasoned captain. No longer will you be left stranded in the dreaded awkward silence!

Body Language and Non-Verbal Cues

Did you know that only 7% of communication is based on the actual words we say? That's right, a whopping 93% of our communication is nonverbal (Lindner, 2023)! Crazy, right?

So, what does this mean for you? It means that paying attention to body language and nonverbal cues is crucial for effective communication.

For example, imagine you're telling your friend about a hilarious joke you heard, but instead of laughing, they're staring blankly at their phone. Ouch, talk about a mood killer! In this case, their body language sends a clear message that they're disinterested and not engaged in the conversation.

On the flip side, if someone is leaning in, making eye contact, and nodding along as you speak, it shows that they're fully present and interested in what you're saying.

Tone Matters

Ever heard the saying, "It's not what you say, but how you say it"? When it comes to communication, your tone of voice, body language, and choice of words can make all the difference.

Picture this: you're asking your friend for a favor, but instead of saying, *"Hey, could you help me out?"* you snap, *"Ugh, why won't you just do this for me?"* It's essentially the same question, but the way you say something can completely change how it's received.

So, when communicating with someone, pay attention to your tone. Speak in a calm, respectful voice, use positive body language, like making eye contact and nodding, and choose your words wisely. It'll make your message much more effective and help you avoid unnecessary drama!

Speak Your Mind, Respectfully

Speaking your mind is like flexing a muscle—the more you use it, the stronger it gets! But here's the thing: While it's important to express your thoughts and opinions, it's equally important to do it respectfully.

Remember, everyone is entitled to their opinion, but that doesn't mean you should disrespect others or spread false information. So, before you speak your mind, take a moment to think:

Is what I'm about to say true?

Is it kind?

Is it necessary?

If the answer is yes, then go ahead and share your thoughts.

Remember to listen to others' perspectives and be open to respectful debate. And if you ever disagree, remember the golden rule: *treat others how you want to be treated.*

To take this a step further, let's touch on assertiveness. Being assertive means expressing your thoughts, feelings, and opinions clearly, confidently, and respectfully. It's like standing up for yourself without stepping on anyone else's toes. Now, let's not confuse assertiveness with aggression. Assertiveness is about being firm but fair, while aggression is more about being forceful and disrespectful.

With a bit of kindness and respect, you can speak your mind while maintaining healthy relationships with those around you. Trust me when I say this is a powerful skill that's highly underrated in today's society. Master the skill of speaking your mind respectfully, and you'll be lightyears ahead of your peers.

When you have something to say, speak up confidently, but remember to do it in a way that considers others' feelings.

Electric Etiquette

In today's digital world, communication doesn't just happen face-to-face. We've got phone calls, texting, emails—you name it! But here's the thing: Just because you're not talking in person doesn't mean manners go out the window.

Whether you're chatting on the phone, sending a text, or composing an email, it's important to remember the golden rule: Treat others with respect and courtesy. That means using polite language, responding promptly (but not too quickly—nobody likes a text bomb!), and thinking twice before hitting send.

Oh, and don't forget about tone! It's easy to misinterpret messages when texting or emailing, so always aim for a friendly and professional tone. And if you're ever unsure how to phrase something or whether it's appropriate to send, just ask yourself, "*Would I say this to my Grandmother's face?*" If the answer is no, then it's probably best to rephrase.

Trust me, a little digital etiquette goes a long way in building positive relationships and avoiding any communication mishaps!

Digital Communication Footprint

Ah, the internet—a magical place where your every move is immortalized for all eternity! It's like having a permanent record that follows you around like a relentless shadow. And trust me, that shadow has a knack for looming over you at the most inconvenient times!

Picture this: you're sitting in a job interview, feeling confident and ready to impress. Suddenly, your potential boss leans in and says, "*So, about that post you made five years ago...*" Cue the internal panic! It's in moments like these that you realize the true power of your digital footprint.

That's why it's crucial to ask yourself one simple question before hitting the "post" button: "*Would I want my parents, future boss, or college admissions officer to see this?*" If the mere thought makes you cringe harder than biting into a wasabi-filled donut, it's probably best to reconsider.

Remember, your online presence is like a digital tattoo—it's a reflection of who you are and can stick with you for a lifetime. So, before you unleash your inner keyboard warrior or share that questionable meme, take a moment to pause and ponder the long-term impact of your digital interactions. Leave a trail that you'll be proud to look back on—one that showcases your wit, wisdom, and impeccable judgment.

Cultural Sensitivity

In one corner of the world, a simple thumbs-up might be a friendly gesture, while in another, it could be as offensive as giving a random stranger a wet willie. And let's not even get started on the minefield of words that sound perfectly innocent in one language but could make a sailor blush in another!

That's why being culturally cognizant is so essential—it's like having a secret decoder ring for human interaction. By understanding and respecting these differences, you can navigate the world like a seasoned explorer without accidentally causing an international incident.

So, whenever you find yourself in a cross-cultural-communication conundrum, show genuine curiosity, ask questions, and be open-minded. Who knows, you might even learn a thing or two about your own culture in the process!

By embracing cultural sensitivity, you'll be able to build bridges instead of walls. You'll create connections with people from all walks of life, and your relationships will be richer and more colorful than a box of crayons.

Empathetic Communication

Picture this: You're chilling with friends, sharing stories, and the vibes are just right. But then, someone opens up about something heavy, something real. Suddenly, it's not just about hanging out anymore—it's about connecting on a whole other level. That's where empathy kicks in, a communication skill we all need in our toolbox.

Empathy isn't just about feeling for someone; it's about stepping into their world—feeling what they feel. It's when you dive deep into their emotions, see through their eyes, and show up with a heart full of understanding and compassion.

Listen—not just to the words they're saying but to the emotions behind them. Notice the way their eyes light up with excitement or how they hesitate when something bothers them. This isn't just about getting where they're coming from; it's about letting them know they're not alone.

Empathy transforms ordinary chats into deeply meaningful exchanges. It's the secret ingredient that strengthens bonds and builds trust. By being empathetic, you're not just hearing people out; you're making them feel heard. So, let's make empathy our go-to, not just because it's nice, but because understanding and supporting each other is what truly connects us.

Difficult Conversations and Conflict Resolution

Let's face it. Conflicts happen. Disagreements are a natural part of life, whether it's with friends, family, or classmates. But here's the good news: Conflicts don't have to be destructive! With the right approach, you can resolve disagreements peacefully and even strengthen your relationships. So, how do you do it?

First, stay calm. Take a deep breath and try to keep your emotions in check. Next, listen actively (like we talked about before). Hear the other person's perspective, and don't interrupt them or get defensive.

When it's your turn, express your thoughts and feelings respectfully, using "I" statements rather than "You" statements to avoid blaming or accusing.

Finally, work together to find a solution that satisfies both parties. Look for common ground, brainstorm ideas, and be open to compromise.

Remember, the goal isn't to "win" the argument like you're some kind of debate champion with a shiny plastic trophy. That's small-minded stuff. It's about finding a resolution that respects everyone's needs and feelings, even if it means admitting that maybe, just maybe, you might be wrong.

By approaching conflicts with empathy, understanding, and a willingness to find common ground, you'll become a pro at resolving conflicts peacefully—and that's definitely a skill worth having!

The Power Of Apology

Saying "I'm sorry" might seem like just two small words, but they pack a big punch when mending friendships and relationships that got a bit rocky. When you mess up or accidentally hurt someone's feelings, owning up to it shows you're mature enough to recognize your mistakes and care enough to set things right. It's about showing you're not too proud to admit you're wrong and that you're serious about keeping your relationships healthy.

An honest apology shows you're taking responsibility and not just brushing off what happened. It tells your friend or whoever you've upset that you get why they're hurt, and you're bothered about it too. Clearing the air can stop minor drama from blowing up into a bigger deal.

Remember, a genuine apology is more than just saying the words; it's about trying to change and not repeating the same mistakes. So, next time you slip up, a simple "I'm sorry" can go a long way. It can fix things you didn't even know were broken and make relationships stronger than they were in the first place.

Feedback

Giving and receiving feedback might not sound like the most exciting part of life, but it's super important for growing and improving at almost anything.

When it's your turn to give feedback, think about how you can help the other person improve. Be constructive, specific, and elaborate on details. It's also crucial to keep your tone friendly and understanding; make it clear you're on their side.

Now, flipping the script: when you're the one getting feedback, it can be tough not to take things personally or feel a bit defensive. The key is listening and seeing feedback as a gift, not a criticism. Someone is taking the time to help you level up. Show you appreciate their insights with a simple *"Thanks for the feedback!"* and think about how you can use their advice to do better next time.

Whether you're giving or receiving feedback, handling feedback well can lead to remarkable improvements and show everyone you're serious about being your best. It's all about using these moments to reflect, learn, and grow—not just in school or sports but in life.

Exiting Conversations Gracefully

All conversations will naturally run their course at some point. It happens, and it's totally okay. Knowing how to exit a conversation smoothly is a must-have skill, especially if you're at a party or just hanging out with friends.

Dropping a friendly "It was great talking to you, but I've got to head out now" or a casual "Let's catch up more later!" helps you make an exit without making things awkward or making anyone feel like they're being ditched.

Being good at talking to people isn't something you're just born with. It takes practice. Each conversation is a chance to get better. Being patient with yourself and willing to learn from each interaction is key. Maybe you'll notice that asking more questions makes people light up, or that keeping your phone in your pocket makes chats more engaging.

As you get the hang of these basic conversational moves, you'll find it way easier to handle any kind of social situation. Whether you're making new friends, talking to teachers, or just ordering pizza over the phone, knowing how to communicate well sets you up for success.

Keep at it, and soon you'll be chatting up a storm, starting and ending conversations smoothly, and rocking your interactions with complete confidence.

ACTIVITY: Active Listening Practice

- Pair up with a friend or family member.
- Choose a topic to discuss. It could be something lighthearted, like your favorite movie, or more meaningful, like personal goals.
- Take turns being the speaker and the listener.
- As the listener, your goal is to practice active listening. This means giving your full attention to the speaker, maintaining eye contact, nodding or using verbal cues to show understanding, and refraining from interrupting.
- As the speaker, share your thoughts on the chosen topic. Try to express yourself clearly and concisely.
- After each round, switch roles so both participants can practice active listening.
- Once both rounds are complete, take a moment to reflect on the experience. Discuss what you found challenging and what you found compelling.
- Encourage each other to continue practicing active listening in daily conversations.

This activity will enhance your active listening abilities and enrich your understanding of the significance of effective communication in fostering robust relationships.

Chapter 3
Money Skills

Financial peace isn't the acquisition of stuff. It's learning to live on less than you make so you can give back and have money to invest. You can't win until you do this.
—Dave Ramsey

Mastering money skills early on can set you up for a lifetime of financial success and freedom. Whether you're saving up for that gaming console that's been calling your name, buying your first car, or even investing in your future, understanding how to manage your money wisely is critical.

Throughout this chapter, we'll cover the basics of money management. How to earn it (legally, of course), save it (without resorting to a diet of ramen noodles), spend it (responsibly, not on that life-sized Yoda statue), and invest it (so you can watch your money grow like a magical beanstalk). By the end, you'll be ready to take on your financial future one dollar at a time.

Understanding the Value of Money

Money isn't just about the bills in your wallet or the digits on a screen. It's much more than that. *Money represents opportunities, options, and your ability to make things happen in life.* The more money you have, the more these things become available to you. Conversely, having less money can limit your choices and opportunities, making you feel trapped. *This is why money is an enormous source of stress for many people.*

Think of money as a tool that enables you to achieve your goals and live the life you want. Whether pursuing higher education, traveling the world, starting a business, or buying a home—money is crucial in making these aspirations a reality.

Achieving financial stability offers a sense of calm and the liberty to chase your interests without the constant concern of struggling to meet your needs. It empowers you to take calculated risks and invest in your future, knowing you have a safety net to fall back on if things don't go as planned.

On the other hand, struggling with financial challenges can be incredibly stressful and limiting. It can hinder your ability to seize opportunities and achieve your long-term goals. That's why it's essential to understand *the true value of money* and manage it wisely. We're going to talk a lot more about how to manage your money, but before you can manage it, first you have to earn it.

Ways To Put Cash In Your Pocket

This section is here to ignite your creativity and initiative, guiding you to identify potential earning opportunities that align with your passions and skills. Whether you're turning a hobby into a cash cow (moo-lah) or filling a need in your community (like becoming the neighborhood's go-to pet-sitter), this guide will inspire you to think outside the box for money-making opportunities.

- **Babysitting:** For those of you who are great with kids, babysitting is a tried-and-true method to earn some dough. This could be your go-to if you're responsible and enjoy hanging out with younger children. Start by watching neighbors' or family friends' kids. Word of mouth can really build your client base here.
- **Lawn Care or Snow Shoveling:** Do you have a knack for outdoor work? Many people don't have the time (or desire) to mow their lawns or shovel their driveways. Offering to take care of these chores can be lucrative, whether it's raking leaves, mowing lawns, or clearing snow. Plus, it's great exercise!
- **Tutoring:** If you're particularly good at a subject like math, science, or English or can play a musical instrument well, why not teach others? Tutoring younger students or peers can be a rewarding way to earn money. You can start with people in your neighborhood or spread the word at your school.
- **Pet Sitting and Dog Walking:** Animal lovers, unite! If you love pets, consider pet sitting or dog walking. Many pet owners need someone to

look after their furry friends while they're at work or on vacation. This job can be fun and relatively easy if you're an animal enthusiast.

- **Selling Crafts or Art:** Are you creative? You can make and sell your creations, whether jewelry, art, crafts or even digital designs. Platforms like Etsy or local craft fairs are great places to start turning your artistic talents into money.
- **Freelance Services:** For the tech-savvy, freelancing in graphic design, web development, or writing can be incredibly profitable. Sites like Fiverr and Upwork allow you to market your skills globally.
- **Social Media Management:** Many local businesses need help to maintain their social media presence. If you know your way around platforms like Instagram, Twitter, or Facebook, offer to manage social media accounts for some cash. It's a great way to use your online skills productively.
- **Part-Time Jobs:** Depending on your age, local businesses like grocery stores, cafes, or retail shops might be looking for part-time help. These jobs can offer regular paychecks, work experience, and sometimes even employee benefits.
- **Car Wash and Detailing:** If you can drive and access car-detailing supplies, offering car washing services can bring in good money. People love having a clean car but might not have the time, desire, or supplies to do it themselves.
- **Virtual Assistant Work:** As businesses move online, many entrepreneurs need help with tasks like data entry, appointment scheduling, and email management. If you're organized and can handle multiple tasks, this could be a perfect gig from the comfort of your home.

Earning your own money isn't just about the cash—it's about independence, responsibility, and learning to manage your finances. So pick one (or a few) of these ideas that sound fun to you and start sharpening those entrepreneurial skills.

Needs vs. Wants

Learning to identify your needs versus wants is like learning to tell the difference between a must-have, like oxygen, and a nice-to-have, like that fifth pair of sneakers. It's a crucial skill for anyone looking to make smarter money moves and keep their bank account in the green.

Needs are your non-negotiables. We're talking about the absolute basics here—food in your belly, a roof over your head, and clothes that prevent you from getting arrested for public indecency. These are the essentials that you really can't skip. Have to have them, can't do without them—these are needs.

Wants are all the extra things in life, vying for your attention and your dollars. This category includes the latest tech gadgets that make your friends go "ooh" and dining out at places where they put parsley on your plate. While these goodies can undoubtedly bring you joy and comfort, they're also the first thing you can ditch when your budget starts to look like a horror movie.

By being clear about what's essential and what's extra, you can manage your finances and stay on track. Cover your needs first, and then, if your wallet allows, sprinkle in some wants.

Impulse Buying

Ah, impulse buying—the art of acquiring something you hadn't planned on, often spurred by the irresistible call of a "limited-time offer" or a midnight shopping spree. Picture this: you're leisurely browsing your favorite online store, and, boom, a trendy jacket appears. It's sleek, it's stylish, and suddenly, you can't imagine life without it, despite a closet already bulging with jackets. Sound familiar? Yep, we've all had those moments.

But hold up before you smash that "buy now" button, take a beat to ponder, "Do I really need this, or is it just a shiny new want?" (remember our talk earlier?) If it's more about want than a need, consider hunting for a bargain or maybe waiting it out until your bank account is more, shall we say, "jacket-ready."

But, to really get control of your spending, what you need is a budget...

Budgeting Basics

A budget is a plan that helps you manage your income and expenses. It's made up of different components, kind of like pieces of a puzzle that fit together to give you a clear picture of where your money is coming from and where it's going.

The main components of a budget include your income, expenses, and savings. Your income is the money you earn, whether it's from a part-time job, an allowance, or any other source. Expenses are the things you spend your money on, like groceries, rent, transportation, and entertainment. And finally, savings are the portion of your income you set aside for future goals or emergencies.

Regarding prioritizing, it's important to cover your needs first — the essential expenses you can't live without, like food, housing, utilities, and transportation.

Once you've taken care of your needs, you can allocate some of your income toward your wants—the things that bring you joy and happiness, like dining out with friends or buying a new set of headphones.

Last but not least, remember savings! Setting aside a portion of your income for savings is crucial for building financial security and achieving your long-term goals, whether saving up for college, a car, or a dream vacation.

Building a Budget

One popular method that can help you structure your budget is called the 50/30/20 rule. Here's how it works (Whiteside, 2022):

- **50% for Needs:** Start by allocating 50% of your income toward your needs. These are the essential expenses that you can't live without, like rent or mortgage payments, utilities, groceries, transportation, and insurance.
- **30% for Wants:** Next, earmark 30% of your income for wants. These are the things that bring you joy and happiness but aren't necessary for survival. This category can include dining out, entertainment, hobbies, and shopping for non-essential items.
- **20% for Savings:** Finally, set aside 20% of your income for savings and financial goals. This could include building an emergency fund, saving for college or a car, investing for retirement, or paying off debt.

Start by listing all your sources of income, whether from a part-time job, an allowance, or any other source. Then, jot down all your monthly expenses, separating them into needs and wants. Once everything is laid out, do the math to see if your spending aligns with the 50/30/20 rule. If not, you may need to adjust your expenses or find ways to increase your income.

Utilizing Budgeting Apps

Budgeting apps are your digital sidekick for managing your money like a pro. These apps are like having a personal finance coach in your pocket, helping you stay on track with your spending and savings goals. For example, YNAB, Plan'it Prom, Mvelopes, and so on. Here's how they can level up your budgeting game:

Simplifying Expense Tracking

Say goodbye to manually jotting down every expense on paper. Budgeting apps make tracking your spending easy by automatically categorizing your transactions. Whether swiping your debit card at the grocery store or ordering takeout online, these apps record where your money is going. This way, you can see at a glance how much you're spending on essentials versus non-essentials and identify areas where you can cut back.

Goal Setting Made Easy

Want to save up for a new phone, a weekend getaway, or even college tuition? Budgeting apps make setting and tracking financial goals a breeze. Input your goal amount and target date, and the app will calculate how much you need to save each month to reach your target. You'll get real-time updates on your progress, motivating you to stay disciplined and stick to your budget.

The Envelope System

Here's how it works: You take your hard-earned money and divide it into different spending categories, like groceries (gotta keep the fridge stocked), entertainment (because Netflix isn't going to watch itself), or clothes (for when you outgrow your pair of lucky socks).

You put a designated amount of cash into each envelope, label them with the category, and boom! You're ready to take on the world, one purchase at a time. When it's time to buy something, you simply reach into the corresponding envelope and use that cash.

Now, here's the catch: once an envelope runs out of money, that's it. Finito. No more spending in that category. It's kind of like a game—and the name of the game is Financial Discipline.

The envelope system helps you stay on track and avoid overspending. It's a simple yet effective way to keep your money in check and make sure you're not blowing your budget on impulse buys.

So, grab some envelopes, label them with your spending categories, and get ready to get a better handle on your finances.

This method is a great way to visualize where your money is going and helps prevent overspending. Plus, it encourages mindful spending since you're using physical cash rather than swiping a card.

Applying Envelope System Principles Digitally

Many budgeting apps like Mvelopes offer a virtual envelope feature where you can allocate funds to different categories within the app. It works like the physical envelopes, but you use digital funds instead of cash.

The digital envelope system is convenient and customizable. It allows you to easily track your spending, set limits for each category, and adjust your budget on the go. Plus, it eliminates the risk of losing cash or dealing with bulky envelopes.

Smart Spending

We all love snagging a good deal, right? But sometimes, going for the cheapest option can cost you more in the long run. It's like this: not all bargains are created equal, and sometimes, splurging a bit on quality can be the more intelligent move.

Quality Over Quantity

Imagine you're trying to decide between 2 pairs of sneakers. One pair is cheap but flimsy, and another is pricier but sturdy. If you go for the cheap pair, you might return for new ones sooner than you think. But if you invest in the sturdy pair, your feet (and wallet) will thank you later when you're not shopping for replacements every few months. If you spend $100 on shoes that last two years instead of $30 on shoes that last three months, you're saving money and hassle in the long run.

Think Long-Term

It's not just about what you're buying; it's about considering the lifespan of what you buy. Take a backpack, for example. If you pick one that's more expensive because it's well-made and has a warranty, it could last through all your high school years and even into college. That's a lot of bang for your buck compared to replacing a cheaper one every year.

Invest in Experiences

Sometimes, the best thing you can spend your money on isn't a thing at all—*it's an experience*! Whether it's a concert, a travel adventure, or a class to learn a new skill, experiences can enrich your life in ways that a new gadget or outfit never will. These memories and skills don't lose value over time; they enhance your knowledge and expand your world!

So next time you're about to make a purchase, pause and consider: is this just a quick thrill, or is it something that will stand the test of time? Will it keep needing to be replaced, or will it last and last?

Sometimes, shelling out a bit more initially can be the move that saves you money and hassle, giving you better quality, longer-lasting satisfaction and, ultimately, more value for your hard-earned cash.

Remember, smart shopping isn't just about finding the lowest price. It's about understanding the true value of things and making good choices for now *and* later.

Financial Quicksand

Debt is when you owe money to someone else, and it can be a lot like quicksand—easy to get into but difficult to escape. While it's tempting to buy now and pay later, accumulating unnecessary debt can quickly spiral out of control, drowning you in interest payments and financial stress.

Whether through credit cards, loans, or installment plans, taking on debt should be carefully considered and reserved for essential purchases like education or a home. Avoiding unnecessary debt means being mindful of your spending habits, distinguishing between wants and needs, and resisting the temptation to overspend beyond your means.

One of the best ways to avoid debt and practice financial discipline is by setting realistic financial goals. Start by identifying what you want to achieve financially. Saving for a car, funding your education, or building an emergency fund. Then, break down these goals into smaller, manageable steps you can work towards over time.

For example, if your goal is to save $1,000 for a new laptop, you might set a target of saving $100 each month. By setting clear goals and creating a plan to achieve them, you'll be more motivated to stick to your budget, resist unnecessary spending, and prioritize saving for the things that matter most to you.

The Importance of Saving

Saving isn't just about setting money aside for unexpected expenses; it's also about planning for the things that bring you joy and fulfillment. Whether you invest in your education, buy a new gadget, or save for a special event, saving allows you to turn your aspirations into reality.

By setting aside a portion of your income for savings, you're preparing for the future and allowing yourself to enjoy life's experiences to the fullest. So, the next time you're tempted to splurge on something frivolous, think about how much more satisfying it will be to save up for something truly meaningful.

Luckily, you don't have to rely solely on guesswork when saving money. Plenty of online tools and calculators, such as Money Fit and My Doh, can help you visualize your savings goals and track your progress over time. These tools allow you to input information like your current savings, monthly contributions, and desired savings goal, then provide you with a clear projection of how long it will take to reach your target.

Whether saving for a short-term goal like a new phone or a long-term goal like retirement, using these tools can help you stay motivated and on track toward achieving your financial aspirations.

The Plastic Jungle

So, you're starting to handle your own money. Exciting, right? As you dive into the world of financial independence, you'll likely come across two main players: debit cards and credit cards. They may look the same, but they play different roles in managing your money.

Debit Cards: Your Direct Line to Your Money

Think of your debit card as a direct pipeline to your bank account. When you swipe or tap this card at the checkout, the cash you spend is pulled straight out of your account. There is no middleman, no borrowing, just your money paying for what you need right then and there. It's straightforward and great for keeping on track with your budget because you can only spend what you have.

Credit Cards: Borrow Now, Pay Later

Cue dramatic music Enter the world of credit cards, where the stakes are high and the temptations are plenty. Credit cards are like having a miniature loan shark in your wallet, except they wear fancy suits and go by names like "Platinum" or "Rewards."

When you use a credit card, you're essentially borrowing money from the issuer, who's fronting the cash on your behalf. It's like having a wealthy uncle who's always willing to lend you money, but with strings attached. You agree to pay back the amount you've borrowed, but here's the catch: if you don't pay off your balance in full each month, Ole Uncle Moneybags will slap you with interest charges faster than you can say "shopaholic."

If you're not careful, those interest charges can pile up faster than dirty laundry in a college dorm room. Suddenly, that $50 pair of shoes you bought on a whim ends up costing you $75 or more. It's like paying a tax for being forgetful or financially irresponsible.

So, while credit cards can be convenient and even rewarding (hello, cashback!), it's crucial to use them wisely. Treat them like a tool, not a toy, and always aim to pay off your balance in full each month.

Why Your Credit Score Matters

And then there's your credit score—a number that follows you around like a GPA for your financial behaviors. This score measures how well you manage debt and how risky it might be for a lender to lend you money. A high credit score can open doors to the nicer things in life, like reasonable rates on car loans, your first apartment, or more favorable credit cards. On the flip side, a low score can make these things harder and more expensive to obtain.

Investments and Compound Interest

You've heard people talk about investing, but what exactly does it mean? Investing is putting your money into something with the hope that it will grow over time.

There are different types of investments, like stocks, bonds, mutual funds, and real estate, each with its own level of risk and potential return. The idea is to choose investments that align with your financial goals and risk tolerance. For you, right now, I would recommend starting with a high-interest savings account. That way, you can start taking advantage of something called "compound interest".

Compound interest is like magic. It's the interest you earn on both your original investment and the interest that's already been earned. In simple terms, it's *interest on top of interest*. Over time, it can turn even a tiny amount of money into a substantial sum.

Example: Compound Interest Over 20 Years

Imagine you put $1,000 into a high-interest savings account and just left it there for 20 years. If the account has an interest rate of 5% per year, here's a simplified look at how your money would grow:

Start with: $1,000

After 20 years with compound interest:

Your initial $1,000 turns into approximately $2,653.30.

This growth happens because each year, you earn interest not just on your original $1,000 *but also on all the interest accumulated from previous years*. By the time you hit 20 years, your money has more than doubled, showing how powerful compound interest can be over time!

To take this example one step further, imagine if you were also to add $100 a month to that same account. Of course, this will be far more relevant once you're earning money regularly, but stay with me on this...

After 20 years of starting with an initial deposit of $1,000, adding $100 every month, and earning a 5% annual interest rate compounded yearly, your savings would grow to approximately $44,316.40.

Of that amount, $19,316.40 is from interest alone!

The key to harnessing the power of compound interest? Start early and be patient. By investing consistently over time and allowing your money to grow, you can take advantage of compounding to build wealth steadily. It's all about delayed gratification. Instead of spending all your money now, you're willing to wait and let it grow, knowing that your future self will thank you.

Wrap-Up

Managing your money wisely is a skill that will benefit you for a lifetime. Stay disciplined and focused, even when that sparkly new gadget is calling your name. And don't be afraid to seek guidance when needed—even the most successful people have mentors! With the right mindset and tools, you can take control of your financial future and build a solid foundation for the life you've always dreamed of.

ACTIVITY: Create Your Personal Budget Blueprint

1. Identify Your Income Sources: Begin by noting down all your income sources, including allowances, part-time jobs, and any other streams of income you might have.

2. List Fixed Expenses: Write out all your regular, recurring expenses, such as school fees, transportation costs, and monthly subscriptions or memberships.

3. Catalog Variable Expenses: Record your fluctuating expenses, which can vary from month to month, like entertainment, dining out, and shopping.

4. Calculate Net Income: Add up all your expenses and subtract the total from your income to determine whether you have a surplus or a deficit.

5. Manage a Surplus: If you find you have extra money after expenses, consider allocating a portion to savings or investing it.

6. Address a Deficit: If expenses exceed income, identify areas to reduce spending or explore options to increase your income.

7. Regularly Review and Adjust: Keep a regular check on your budget, updating and adjusting as necessary to ensure you stay aligned with your financial goals.

Chapter 4
Emotional Skills

When dealing with people, remember you are not dealing with creatures of logic but with creatures of emotion.
—Dale Carnegie

Emotions are like the unpredictable weather of our inner world, turning our days sunny or stormy without much warning. Ever felt butterflies doing aerobics in your stomach before a big event? Or maybe experienced the sensation of your heart taking the elevator straight to the basement when something goes wrong? Yep, those are your emotions showing up in full force. They're our body's dramatic way of responding to life's ups and downs—whether it's a surprise party, a horror movie, or just another day of bewildering plot twists in the ongoing story of our lives.

Understanding our emotions helps us make sense of what we're feeling and why we're feeling it. When we can name our emotions—like happiness, anger, sadness, or fear, it's like putting labels on different jars in our emotional pantry. When we can do that, it's the beginning of something called "Emotional Intelligence."

Emotional Intelligence

Have you ever heard the phrase "heart and mind"? Emotional intelligence is the magic that happens when your heart and mind work together. It's a powerful type of awareness that can guide our thoughts and actions.

Emotional intelligence comprises of four skills (Chefalo, 2023):

1. Self-awareness: Knowing how and why you feel that way.

2. Self-regulation: Managing your emotions, even when things get tough.

3. Social awareness: This involves recognizing and empathizing with the feelings and experiences of others.

4. Relationship management: Managing relationships involves leveraging your emotional intelligence to navigate social interactions and communicate proficiently.

These skills aren't just helpful—they're essential for getting along in the world. They help us build healthy relationships, make good decisions, and bounce back from challenges stronger than before.

So, by understanding our emotions and honing our emotional intelligence, we become the masters of our emotional universe!

Managing Emotions

Imagine you're at the movies, and suddenly, the music gets intense, your heart starts racing, and your palms get sweaty. What's happening? What you're feeling is a reaction to *stress*. So, the next time you find yourself swept up in a whirlwind of emotions, imagine you're watching a captivating movie starring none other than yourself. Take a step back, observe the storyline unfolding, and remember that you hold the power to influence the outcome.

Emotions can be pretty sneaky. Sometimes, they come on strong, like when you're excited about something extraordinary. Other times, they creep up quietly, like when you're feeling a little down for no apparent reason.

To get a handle on our emotions, we first need to recognize what we're feeling. Are you feeling angry, sad, happy, or maybe a mix of everything? Once we've identified our emotions, it's time to tackle them head-on. If you're feeling overwhelmed by stress, take a breather. Find a quiet spot, close your eyes, and take some deep breaths. Trust me, it works wonders!

Stress is like a little alarm bell going off in your brain, telling you something's up. But here's the thing: stress isn't always bad. Sometimes, it can motivate us to tackle challenges and get stuff done. The key is knowing when stress is helping us and when it's holding us back.

When stress starts to feel like a heavy backpack weighing you down, it's time to take action. It could be talking to a friend, going for a walk, or practicing mindfulness to calm your mind. And if stress starts to pile up, don't hesitate to reach out for help.

Coping Strategies

In the hustle and bustle of teenage life, stress can creep up on you like a ninja in the night. Before you know it, your mind is racing faster than a caffeinated squirrel, and you're wondering how you'll ever find a moment of peace. But fear not, dear reader, for mindfulness is here to save the day!

Mindfulness is the art of being fully present and aware of your thoughts, feelings, and surroundings without getting caught up in the drama. It's like pressing the pause button on the chaos and taking a step back to observe the madness with a sense of calm and clarity.

One of the simplest and most effective mindfulness techniques is deep breathing. Find a quiet spot where you can sit comfortably, close your eyes, and take a deep breath. Inhale slowly through your nose, hold the breath for a moment, then exhale slowly through your mouth—releasing all the tension and stress you've been holding onto. Repeat this process several times, focusing on the sensation of the breath moving in and out of your body. You might feel a bit silly at first, but trust me, your mind will thank you for the much-needed break.

If sitting still isn't your thing, don't worry! Exercise is a fantastic way to manage stress. When you get moving, your brain mixes up a potent cocktail of feel-good chemicals called endorphins, which can help you feel energized and ready to tackle any challenge. So, put on your favorite workout gear, crank up some motivating tunes, and get your sweat on. Whether you're running, dancing, or practicing martial arts, exercise is a surefire way to show stress who's boss. Embrace the power of physical activity, and you'll soon find yourself grinning from ear to ear, ready to take on the world.

For the creative souls out there, engaging in activities like drawing, writing, or playing music can be incredibly therapeutic. When you lose yourself in the flow of creation, it's like giving your mind a vacation from the daily grind. So, grab your tools of choice and let your imagination run wild. Who knows, you might just create a masterpiece that rivals the Mona Lisa (or at least a stick figure that could pass for abstract art).

So, take a deep breath, embrace the present moment, and remember that stress doesn't stand a chance against the power of mindfulness. And if all else fails, just remember: it's always okay to laugh at the absurdity of it all.

Building Emotional Resilience

Resilience is the ability to spring back from tough times like a champ. But guess what? It's not something you're born with; it's like a muscle that gets stronger with practice.

First, embrace challenges like a bear hug from your overly affectionate aunt. Instead of running away faster than a kid from a steaming plate of asparagus, face those obstacles head-on with a grin and a "bring it on" attitude. Every hurdle you encounter is a chance to grow, learn, and become more resilient.

By the way—being resilient doesn't mean you *never fail*—ha, who does that anyways? It means you fail so epically that your blooper reel could go viral on YouTube. But then you dust yourself off and give it another go... this time armed with better intel from your previous attempt. Remember, failure is just a stepping stone on the path to success.

Overcoming Fear

Fear—the sneaky little gremlin that loves to hold us back. But here's the secret: fear only has power if you let it. It's time to take back control and face your fears like a warrior.

Start by identifying your fears. What makes your palms sweaty and your heart race? Write them down and spotlight them. Sometimes, just acknowledging your fears can remove their power.

Next, separate rational fears from irrational ones. Sure, being afraid of jumping out of a plane without a parachute is pretty logical. *I feel sweaty just thinking about it*. But being terrified of speaking up in class? Not so much. Learn to distinguish between genuine danger and imaginary monsters under the bed.

And finally, take action. Don't let fear call the shots. Show it who's boss! Step out of your comfort zone, one tiny step at a time. With each brave move, you'll chip away at fear's armor until it crumbles away to nothing.

Coping With Loss

Whether it's saying goodbye to a loved one, a friendship, or a cherished dream, loss is a tough pill to swallow. But guess what? You're not alone, and there are ways to navigate the challenging emotions associated with grief.

First things first, give yourself permission to feel. Grief is messy, and it's OK to ride the emotional rollercoaster. Allow yourself to cry, scream, or even laugh. It's all part of the healing process.

Next, lean on your support system. Surround yourself with people who lift you up and provide a shoulder to lean on when times get tough. Whether it's family, friends, or a trusted adult, don't hesitate to ask for help.

And remember, healing takes time. There's no right or wrong way to grieve, so be gentle with yourself as you navigate the ups and downs. Take each day as it comes, and trust that with time, the pain will ease, and brighter days will come again.

Always remember this simple message:

You're stronger than you think you are!

You're also never alone on this journey. With love, support, and a sprinkle of resilience, you can weather any storm.

Self-Development & Forgiveness

Picture this: you muster up the courage to ask your crush to the school dance, only to hear a polite "no" in response. Ouch, right? Rejection stings, but here's the silver lining: it's not the end of the world. In fact, it's a golden opportunity for growth.

How so? Well, rejection teaches us resilience. It toughens our skin and strengthens our resolve to keep pushing forward, no matter the odds. So, dust yourself off instead of wallowing in self-pity, and hold your head high. Your worth isn't defined by one rejection. It's defined by how you bounce back from it.

Speaking of bouncing back, let's talk about forgiveness. Holding onto grudges is like carrying around a backpack full of rocks—it weighs you down and prevents you from moving forward. But forgiveness? It's like setting down that heavy burden and freeing yourself from its weight.

Forgiveness doesn't involve justifying someone's actions or erasing the memory of what occurred. It entails liberating yourself from the hold of anger and bitterness, creating room for healing and personal development. So, take a deep breath, let go of the past, and step into the future with a lighter heart.

Now, let's turn our attention inward and shine a spotlight on the most important relationship of all—the one we have with ourselves. Self-love isn't just about pampering yourself with bubble baths and chocolate (although those things are pretty great). It's about accepting yourself, flaws and all, and treating yourself with kindness and compassion.

So, next time you catch yourself criticizing your reflection in the mirror or doubting your worth, pause for a moment and challenge those negative thoughts. Replace them with affirmations of self-love and appreciation. Try this:

> *I am enough just as I am, and I have*
> *the power to make my dreams a reality.*
> -You

Positive Outlook

Imagine yourself waking up in the morning, and instead of reaching for your phone to scroll through social media, you take a deep breath and think of three things you're grateful for.

It could be as simple as the warmth of sunlight streaming through your window, the fact that you have a soft bed to sleep in with a roof over your head, or maybe the deep gratitude for having been granted another day of life on this beautiful planet. As you can see, there are countless "ordinary" things surrounding us that we have to be genuinely grateful for. Taking the time to recognize them contributes hugely to our outlook on life.

Why bother with gratitude? Well, my friends, it's like hitting the reset button on your mindset. By focusing on the good stuff, you train your brain to see the silver linings, even on cloudy days. Plus, studies show that practicing gratitude can boost your mood, improve your sleep, and even strengthen your relationships (Reid, 2024). Talk about a win-win!

It's all too easy to get caught up in the comparison game—scrolling through social media, wishing you had someone else's life or possessions. But here's the truth: Comparing yourself to others is like trying to fit a square peg into a round hole. It just doesn't work.

Instead, focus on what you have, not what you lack. Savor the small joys in life, like sharing a laugh with friends, enjoying your favorite meal, or cuddling up with a good book.

Remember, happiness isn't about having more; it's about appreciating what you already have. So, let's raise a toast to the little things that make life oh-so-sweet!

Empathy and Integrity

These twin virtues, when cultivated and practiced, have the power to transform our relationships, our communities, and our world.

Empathy, at its core, is the ability to understand and share the feelings of another. It is the capacity to step into someone else's shoes, to see the world through their eyes, and to feel their joys and sorrows as if they were your own. When we empathize with others, we create a bridge of understanding that spans the gaps of difference and division.

Imagine a world without empathy. It would be a cold, harsh place where people are disconnected from one another, unable to relate to each other's experiences or emotions. In such a world, we would be trapped in our own narrow perspectives, unable to grow or learn from those around us.

But when we embrace empathy, we open ourselves up to the richness and diversity of human experience. We learn to listen deeply, to validate others' feelings, and to offer support and compassion without judgment. We recognize that everyone has their own unique struggles and triumphs, and we celebrate the common humanity that binds us all together.

Integrity, on the other hand, is the steadfast adherence to moral and ethical principles. It is the unwavering commitment to doing what is right, even when it is difficult or unpopular. When we act with integrity, we align our actions with our values and beliefs, creating a sense of inner harmony and purpose.

In a world that often seems to reward deception and self-interest, integrity can feel like a rare and precious commodity. It takes courage and strength of character to stand up for what you believe in, especially when faced with pressure to compromise your values.

But when we cultivate integrity, we build trust and respect with those around us. We become a beacon of honesty and reliability, someone that others can count on to do the right thing. We inspire others to hold themselves to a higher standard, creating a ripple effect of positive change in our communities.

Empathy and integrity are not just abstract ideals – they are essential skills for navigating the complexities of life. In our personal relationships, they help us to build deeper, more meaningful connections with others. In our professional lives, they enable us to collaborate effectively, resolve conflicts, and make ethical decisions that benefit the greater good.

When we bring empathy and integrity together, we create a powerful synergy that can transform the world around us. We become agents of compassion and justice, working to create a society that values the dignity and worth of every human being.

So listen with an open heart and mind. Act with courage and conviction. Be the change you wish to see in the world, one small act of kindness and one principled stand at a time. In doing so, you not only enrich your own life, but you help create a brighter, more compassionate future for all.

Encouragment VS Manipulation

Supportive encouragement is lifting others up, cheering them on, and helping them reach their goals. It's like being the wind beneath their wings, giving them the boost they need to soar to new heights. Imagine you're a gardener tending to a delicate plant. You provide the right environment, nourishment, and support, allowing it to grow and thrive at its own pace. That's the essence of supportive encouragement. It's about fostering growth, nurturing potential, and celebrating each individual's unique journey.

On the flip side, manipulative behavior is like trying to steer someone else's ship without their consent. It's about controlling or pressuring others to do what you want, even if it's not in their best interest.

For instance, let's say you have a friend who always insists on picking the movie every time you hang out, ignoring your preferences completely. They might use guilt-tripping tactics or subtle persuasion to make you feel like your choices don't matter. Instead of considering your feelings, they prioritize their own desires, leaving you feeling sidelined and unheard. That's an example of manipulative behavior, where someone tries to control the situation for their benefit without considering how it affects others.

So, instead of manipulating, let's focus on empowering others to make their own choices and supporting them every step of the way.

Self-Control and Responsibility

Imagine it's late at night, and you're 5 hours deep into a video game marathon, but that little voice in your head reminds you of the big test first thing in the morning. That's your opportunity to practice a bit of self-control.

Self-control is about resisting short-term temptations that can undermine long-term goals. It takes work, especially when what you want in the moment feels urgent and convincing.

But here's a trick:

1. Hit the pause button.

2. Take a deep breath.

3. Think about the consequences.

Choosing wisely in these moments might seem like a small thing, but it adds up. Every time you exercise self-control, you're not just avoiding a potential mess but *also building the mental muscle that makes you stronger in facing more significant future challenges*. And let's be honest: If you can trust yourself to make the right choice—that's a huge win!

So next time you're in a bind, remember: a moment of patience can save you a lot of stress and trouble down the line. Exercising self-control now will pay off big time, helping you steer your life in the direction you want to go.

No Excuses

Before we close out this chapter, let's get real about something we've all done before: *make excuses*. You know the drill—blaming the dog for chewing on your homework or insisting you're too swamped to take out the trash. Those might seem like little fibs, but here's the hard truth: making excuses doesn't fix anything.

It's like tossing your problems into a closet and slamming the door shut. Out of sight for now, but definitely not out of mind. Those pesky issues will keep banging on the door, demanding attention like a toddler who's just discovered the joy of pots and pans.

Rather than playing the blame game or crafting creative excuses, it's time to step up and own our actions. This means if you drop the ball, own up to it. Did you make a mistake? Apologize sincerely. Forgot to do your part of a group project? Don't point fingers or dream up reasons why. It's on you to make it right. Taking responsibility might feel tough at first, especially if you're used to deflecting with excuses, but it's a game-changer.

Owning up to what you've done shows real maturity. It proves you're strong enough to face the consequences and intelligent enough to learn from them. Plus, it builds trust. When people know you're someone who admits mistakes and tries to fix them, they respect and rely on you more.

So, as we wrap up, remember: ditching the excuses and embracing responsibility not only clears your conscience but also paves the way for genuine growth and stronger relationships. It's a bold move towards becoming the best version of yourself.

ACTIVITY: Emotion Journal

Grab a notebook and pen; it's time to start your emotion journal! Take a few minutes each day to jot down how you're feeling and why. Was it something exciting that happened at school? Or a frustrating moment with a friend?

At the end of the week, review your entries and look for patterns. Do certain activities or people tend to trigger specific emotions? Understanding these patterns can help you manage your feelings better in the future.

Plus, expressing your emotions through writing can be super therapeutic. So, as you embark on this journey of self-discovery, remember that your emotion journal is more than just a collection of words—it's a powerful tool for growth and healing. Embrace the process wholeheartedly, and let your journal guide you toward a deeper understanding of yourself and your emotions.

Chapter 5
Cooking Skills

Good food is very often, even most often, simple food.
— Anthony Bourdain

In this chapter, we'll dive into the magical world of cooking, where spatulas are your wands and aprons are your capes. We'll start by conquering simple recipes, like Boiled Water (it's a milestone for some, trust me).

Then, we'll graduate to creating *real* culinary masterpieces from proven recipes that will make your taste buds do a happy dance. You'll even learn how to experiment with various ingredients to create dishes of your very own design. Who knows, you might discover a method for turning a turnip into something edible!

But cooking isn't just about filling your belly; it's about the warm and fuzzy feelings that come with preparing healthy meals from scratch. By the end of this chapter, you'll be well on your way to becoming a master chef, or at least a master of not setting the kitchen on fire.

Why Cook?

Cooking is really about so much more than just filling your belly. It can be a fantastic way to bond with friends and family. Imagine hosting a dinner party or cooking a meal together. It's not just about the food; it's about the memories you create and about finding out which of your friends is brave enough to try your experimental dishes. But most importantly, learning to cook gives you a valuable life skill that you'll carry with you forever.

It's also a way to take charge of your health by cooking "from scratch"—because, let's face it, not all ingredients that go into processed foods are good for us—or even pronounceable. I mean, who really wants a side of zylophenitroxy-chlorolechantriphendrobenzamide.

Whether you're living on your own for the first time or just craving something tasty on a lazy Sunday afternoon, mastering the kitchen means you're always just a whisk away from a delicious, healthy meal.

Safety First

First things first, why is kitchen safety such a big deal? Well, think about all the things that could go wrong when cooking—burns, cuts, fires—you name it. Knowing how to stay safe in the kitchen can help prevent accidents and keep you and your loved ones out of harm's way.

So, how can you stay safe while cooking up a storm? Here are a few tips to keep in mind:

- Always wash your hands before and after handling food. This helps prevent the spread of germs and keeps your food safe to eat.
- Pay attention to what you're doing. It's easy to get distracted, especially when chatting with friends or listening to music while cooking.
- Use kitchen tools and equipment properly. That means knowing how to use knives safely, keeping pot handles turned away from the stove's edge, and using oven mitts when handling hot pots and pans.
- Last but not least, don't be afraid to ask for help if needed. Whether you're unsure how to use a particular kitchen gadget or feel overwhelmed by a recipe, there's no shame in asking for help.

Essential Kitchen Tools and Equipment

There are a lot of tools and utensils required for cooking.

Knives, cutting boards, mixing bowls, measuring cups, measuring spoons, whisk, spatula, ladle, tongs, saucepan, frying pan, baking sheet, colander, vegetable peeler, grater, kitchen shears, rolling pin, can opener, unicorn horn sharpener...

Just kidding about that last one, but you get the idea.

You might be thinking, "Do I really need all this stuff?" Well, the short answer is yes. Here are the basics and why you need them:

Knives

A good set of knives is like a chef's best friend. You'll want a chef's knife for chopping, slicing, and dicing; a paring knife for smaller tasks like peeling fruits and veggies; and a serrated knife for slicing bread and delicate items like tomatoes.

Cutting Boards

These are essential for protecting your countertops and food from germs. Opt for ones made of wood or plastic that are easily cleaned.

Pots & Pans

You'll want a few different-sized pots for boiling pasta, making soups, and cooking grains. Don't forget about frying pans for sautéing veggies, frying eggs, and searing meats.

Measuring Cups

Other must-have tools include measuring cups and spoons for accurately measuring ingredients, mixing bowls for combining ingredients, and a whisk for beating eggs and mixing batters.

Helpful Gadgets

Lastly, let's not forget about gadgets like ladles, tongs, and spatulas for flipping, turning, and serving food. Oh, and a can opener for, well, you know!

Understanding Cooking Methods

Cooking is like a science; each method brings out different flavors and textures in your food. Here are some of the most common techniques you'll encounter:

Grilling: Grilling is cooking over an open flame or hot coals. It's perfect for cooking meats, veggies, and even fruits like pineapple and peaches. Grilling gives food a smoky flavor and those beautiful grill marks we love.

Roasting: Roasting involves cooking food in the oven at high heat. It's great for meats, poultry, and veggies like potatoes and carrots. Roasting caramelizes the sugars in food, giving it a rich flavor and crispy texture.

Sauteing: Sauteing is a quick cooking method that involves cooking food in oil or butter over high heat. It's perfect for veggies, seafood, and thinly sliced meats. Sauteing gives food a golden-brown color and locks in flavor.

Boiling: Boiling is when you cook food in boiling water. It's great for pasta, rice, and veggies like broccoli and green beans. Boiling cooks food quickly and evenly, but be careful not to overcook!

Steaming: Steaming involves cooking food over boiling water without submerging it. It's perfect for delicate foods like fish, shellfish, and veggies. Steaming preserves nutrients and natural flavors without adding any extra fat.

Baking: Baking is cooking food in the oven surrounded by dry heat. It's perfect for bread, cakes, cookies, and casseroles. Baking creates a golden crust and soft interior, giving food that irresistible homemade taste.

Keep A Clean Kitchen

Firstly, cleanliness in the kitchen helps prevent foodborne illnesses. Bacteria love to hang out in dirty areas. If they get into your food, they can make you very sick. So, washing your hands before and after handling food and regularly cleaning countertops, cutting boards, and utensils can help keep those germs at bay.

Secondly, a clean kitchen makes cooking a lot easier and more enjoyable. Imagine chopping veggies on a cluttered countertop or cooking on a dirty stove. Not fun, right? Keeping your cooking area clean and organized gives you more space to work and less stress while preparing meals.

Now, here are some tips to help you maintain a clean kitchen:

Wash dishes as you go: Don't let dirty dishes pile up in the sink. Wash them or load them into the dishwasher as soon as you're done using them. It'll make cleanup a breeze!

Wipe up spills immediately: Spills happen, but leaving them to sit can lead to stains and sticky messes. Keep a clean cloth or sponge handy to wipe up spills as soon as they occur.

Empty the trash regularly: Nobody likes a smelly kitchen! Make sure to empty the trash bin regularly to keep odors at bay and prevent pests from making themselves at home.

Sweep and mop the floor: Crumbs and spills can accumulate on the floor, so give it a quick sweep and mop regularly to keep it clean and hygienic.

Reading and Following Recipes

Understanding a recipe is key to cooking success. Recipes lay out the ingredients you need and the steps you need to take to turn those ingredients into a tasty dish. So, before you start cooking, take a moment to read through the recipe from start to finish. Pay attention to the ingredients, measurements, and cooking methods. This will help you understand what you're about to make and avoid any surprises along the way.

Now, when it comes to following a recipe, accuracy is key. Here are some tips to help you follow recipes accurately:

Follow the steps in order: Recipes are like building blocks — each step builds upon the last. So, follow the instructions in the order they're given to achieve the best results.

Prep ingredients before you start: Chop, dice, and prep all your ingredients before cooking. This will make the process smoother and help you stay organized.

Measure ingredients correctly: Use measuring cups and spoons to ensure you add the right amount of each ingredient. Too much or too little can throw off the flavor and texture of your dish.

Pay attention to cooking times and temperatures: Keep an eye on the clock and set a timer to ensure you don't overcook or undercook your dish.

By taking the time to read and accurately follow recipes, you'll be well on your way to becoming a confident and skilled cook.

Substituting Ingredients

Inevitably, you'll eventually find yourself right in the middle of cooking up a tasty dish, only to realize you're missing a key ingredient. Don't panic! Ingredient substitutions to the rescue!

Here's the deal: ingredient substitutions involve swapping out one ingredient for another that serves a similar purpose in the recipe.

For example, if a recipe calls for buttermilk but you don't have any on hand, you can make your own by adding a tablespoon of lemon juice or vinegar to regular milk and letting it sit for a few minutes to curdle. Voila! Instant buttermilk substitute.

Now, when it comes to adapting recipes based on available ingredients, it's all about getting creative. Let's say a recipe calls for broccoli, but you have cauliflower instead. No problem! Cauliflower can easily step in for broccoli in many recipes, like stir-fries or casseroles.

Here are some tips for successful ingredient substitutions:

Understand the ingredient's role: Is it providing moisture, texture, flavor, or leavening? This will help you choose a suitable substitute.

Keep flavor profiles in mind: Choose substitutes that complement the other flavors in the dish. For example, if a recipe calls for rosemary but you're out, thyme or oregano could work well as substitutes.

Be flexible and experiment: Don't be afraid to get creative and try new things. Who knows, you might discover a flavor combination you love!

Simple Beginner Recipes

Let's whip up some magic in the kitchen and gain some valuable cooking experience with some easy-to-follow recipes!

Mac and Cheese

First, we have everyone's favorite comfort food: creamy mac and cheese (Gallagher & Gallagher, n.d.). Here's what you'll need:

Ingredients:

- 1 pound dried pasta (like elbow macaroni, shells, or penne)

- 5 tablespoons unsalted butter

- 1 pound white cheddar cheese (shredded)

- 5 cups milk (whole or 2% reduced fat)

- 4 ounces cream cheese (optional)

- 5 tablespoons all-purpose flour

- 1/2 teaspoon fresh ground black pepper

- 1/2 teaspoon fine sea salt (plus more to taste)

Instructions:

1. Cook the pasta according to package directions. Drain & set aside.

2. Now, let's make that creamy cheese sauce. Melt butter in a large pot over medium heat, then add flour and whisk until it's light brown and smells amazing.

3. Slowly pour in warm milk while whisking constantly until the sauce thickens and simmers.

4. Reduce the heat, then stir in cheddar and cream cheeses, salt, and pepper until smooth.

5. Add the cooked pasta to the sauce, stir well, and let it sit covered for 5 minutes. Then, it's ready to serve!

If you're feeling extra fancy, you can turn this into baked mac and cheese by transferring it to a baking dish, adding breadcrumbs and more cheese on top, and then baking it until golden brown and bubbly.

Chocolate Pudding Cake

Next on the list, we have a decadent chocolate pudding cake that's sure to satisfy your sweet tooth (Martha, 2014):

Ingredients:

- 1 1/4 cups granulated sugar

- 1/2 cup unsweetened cocoa powder

- 1 cup all-purpose flour

- 1/2 cup milk

- 2 teaspoons baking powder

- 1/3 cup unsalted butter (melted)

- 1/4 teaspoon salt

- 1/2 cup packed brown sugar

- 1 1/2 teaspoons vanilla extract

- 1 1/4 cups hot water

- vanilla ice cream (optional for serving)

Instructions:

1. Preheat your oven to 350°F and grease a 2-quart ceramic dish or a 9-inch square baking pan.

2. Combine granulated sugar, flour, baking powder, and salt in a mixing bowl.

3. Stir in milk, melted butter, and vanilla until smooth, then spread the batter in the prepared dish.

4. In another bowl, mix brown sugar and cocoa powder, then sprinkle this over the batter.

5. Pour hot water over the top of the batter, but don't stir.

6. Bake until set in the center, about 350°F for 40 minutes.

7. Let it cool for 15 minutes, then scoop into bowls, topping with ice cream if desired.

Classic Egg Salad

And last but not least, let's whip up a classic egg salad (Martha, 2020):

Ingredients:

- 4 quarts water

- 6 eggs

- 4 tablespoons mayonnaise

- 1 tablespoon white vinegar

- Pinch of salt

- Pinch of white pepper

Instructions:

1. Boil the eggs for 5 minutes, then let them sit in hot water for 13 minutes.

2. Peel and chop the eggs, then mix with mayonnaise, vinegar, salt, and pepper.

3. Chill in the fridge, then serve with lettuce and bread.

There, you have some simple yet delicious recipes to try out in your kitchen! Enjoy cooking, and don't forget to share your culinary creations with friends and family.

Keep in mind one of the most incredible things about cooking:

Cooking is the only art form where you get to eat your mistakes—so don't be afraid to try new things, experiment, and have fun. It's all part of the learning experience.

Planning and Organizing Meals

Trust me, meal planning is not as daunting as it sounds, and it can make your life much easier.

First things first, why is meal planning important? Well, think about it like this: When you plan your meals ahead of time, you're saving time and money and making healthier choices. Instead of scrambling last minute and settling for fast food or unhealthy snacks, you'll have nutritious meals ready to go.

Now, let's get into some tips for organizing your meals efficiently:

- Start by making a weekly meal plan. Sit down for a few minutes at the beginning of each week and jot down what you want to eat for breakfast, lunch, and dinner each day. Don't forget about snacks too!
- Take inventory of what you already have. Before heading to the grocery store, check your fridge, freezer, and pantry to see what ingredients you already have. This will help you avoid buying duplicates and save you money.
- Get creative with leftovers. Instead of letting leftover food go to waste, plan to incorporate it into future meals. For example, suppose you roast a chicken for dinner one night. In that case, you can use the leftover meat to make chicken salad sandwiches or add it to a pasta dish later in the week.
- Keep it simple. You don't have to make elaborate meals every night of the week. Stick to easy-to-make recipes that use simple ingredients, especially if you're short on time.
- Prep ahead of time. Spend some time on the weekends chopping vegetables, cooking grains, and marinating meats. This will make cooking during the week a breeze and help you stay on track with your meal plan.

Understanding Food Labels and Ingredients

So, why should you turn into a label sleuth? These little panels on every store-bought food item tell you what makes up the food inside the package. For instance, they tell you exactly how much sugar, fat, and sodium is hidden in your favorite snacks, helping you make choices that might even impress your doctor.

Sugar: Keep an eye out for added sugars in products like soda, candy, and packaged snacks. Too much sugar can contribute to weight gain and other health issues, so it's important to limit your intake.

Fat: Different types of fats have varying effects on your health. While fats from sources like nuts and avocados can be beneficial in moderation, trans fats, for instance, can elevate your chances of developing heart disease. Look for products with healthier fats and try to limit your intake of saturated and trans fats.

Sodium: High sodium levels can raise your blood pressure and increase your risk of heart disease. Try to choose lower-sodium options whenever possible, and be mindful of how much salt you add to your food when cooking at home.

Ingredients you can't pronounce: If you come across a long list of ingredients with names you can't pronounce, it might be a sign that the product is highly processed. PRO TIP: If it sounds more like a spell from Harry Potter than food, it's probably best to avoid eating it.

The Impact of Diet on Health

Have you ever heard the saying, "You are what you eat"? Well, there's a lot of truth to that! The food we put into our bodies significantly affects how we feel and function daily.

First, let's discuss how diet affects overall health. Eating a balanced diet that includes plenty of fruits, vegetables, whole grains, and lean proteins provides your body with the nutrients it needs to function properly. These nutrients help support energy levels, immune function, and even mood.

On the flip side, a diet high in processed foods, sugary snacks, and unhealthy fats can negatively affect your health. It can lead to things like weight gain, fatigue, and an increased risk of chronic diseases like diabetes and heart disease.

That's where cooking nutritious meals comes in. When you cook your own meals at home, you have control over what goes into them. Opt for fresh, whole ingredients to avoid added sugars, artificial additives, and unhealthy fats commonly present in processed foods.

So, next time you're thinking about what to eat, remember the impact that your diet can have on your health. You'll set yourself up for a happier, healthier life by cooking nutritious meals and making smart food choices.

Kitchen Emergencies

Cooking is all about crafting tasty dishes and having fun, but let's face it, it's also about perfecting your quick reflexes for when things go sideways. Being prepared for those unexpected kitchen mishaps is just as crucial. Whether it's a minor burn from a rogue splash of sauce or a serious grease fire that wants to audition for a spot in a disaster movie, knowing how to handle these emergencies can keep a small problem from turning into a dinner party anecdote that your friends will never let you live down.

Fire Safety: If you find yourself facing a grease fire, forget about using water. It could make things worse by spreading the flames. Instead, keep your cool and quickly smother the flames by covering the pan with a lid and turning off the burner. If the fire refuses to go out or grows too large, it's time to call 911 right away.

Dealing with Cuts and Burns: Accidents like cuts and burns can happen quickly. If you get a cut, rinse it under cool water and bandage it to keep it clean. For burns, cool the area under running water and gently cover it with a clean dressing. If the burn is really bad or covers a large area, don't hesitate to seek medical help.

First Aid Kit Essentials: Every kitchen should have a first aid kit that's easy to get to and stocked with essentials like bandages, antiseptic wipes, and burn cream. Make sure everyone knows where it is and how to use what's inside. Being prepared isn't just responsible—it's a pro move.

By being informed and ready for anything, you can keep your culinary adventures safe and focus more on the fun and creativity of cooking.

Kitchen Etiquette

When it comes to cooking, it's not only about following recipes and mastering culinary skills; it's also about being respectful and considerate in shared cooking spaces. Whether you're cooking with family, friends, or roommates, good kitchen etiquette can go a long way in creating a positive cooking experience for everyone involved.

First off, it's essential to clean up after yourself. Nobody likes to walk into a messy kitchen, so be sure to wash your dishes, wipe down countertops, and put away ingredients and utensils when you're done cooking. This helps maintain a clean and organized cooking environment for everyone to enjoy.

Next, be mindful of others' cooking preferences and dietary restrictions. If you're cooking for a group, take the time to ask if anyone has any food allergies or dietary restrictions – you don't want to accidentally serve your gluten-free friend a heaping plate of wheat spaghetti! If you've got a vegan in the mix, don't just hand them a head of lettuce and call it a day. Get creative and whip up some tasty plant-based dish that'll make even the most die-hard carnivores jealous.

Wrap-Up

Remember, conquering the kitchen is less about perfection and more about the journey of flavors, laughter, and occasional mishaps. Whether you're wrestling with your first complicated recipe or rescuing a dish on the brink of disaster, embrace each challenge with a dash of humor and a sprinkle of determination. So keep your spirit high and your curiosity alive; with each meal, you're not just filling plates but also crafting stories and honing a skill that will enrich your life in countless ways.

ACTIVITY: The Recipe Remix Challenge

Objective: Enhance your culinary creativity and technical skills by transforming a classic dish into something uniquely yours.

Materials List:

1. Classic Recipe: Choose a well-known dish to serve as the foundation. This could be something like spaghetti Bolognese, grilled cheese sandwich, or apple pie.

2. Additional Ingredients: Encourage creativity by selecting three to five ingredients not typically used in the classic recipe. These could include an exotic spice, an unusual vegetable, or a cheese you've never tried.

3. Timer: Give yourself a specific time frame to complete the challenge, such as one hour. This will encourage quick thinking and decision-making.

Make It Your Own:

Cook your remixed dish, focusing on integrating the new ingredients seamlessly with the old recipe. Once done, take a moment to plate your creation appealingly.

Reflection and Sharing:

- **Taste Test:** After cooking, sit down and taste your creation. Think about what worked and what could be improved.

- **Share Your Dish:** Share your dish with family or friends. Get feedback on your innovation and presentation.

- **Document It:** Take photos or even jot down the new recipe. Reflect on your cooking process and the flavors you created.

This challenge tests your ability to think outside the box and helps build confidence in your cooking abilities. It's a fun way to experiment with flavors and learn about balancing different ingredients in a dish. Plus, it's an excellent opportunity to add a personal touch to classic meals and discover a new favorite recipe!

Chapter 6
Personal Skills

Life is 10% what happens to us and 90% how we react to it.
—Charles R. Swindoll

This chapter is about setting you up with simple personal skills to help you better navigate life's twists and turns. From being punctual to taking responsibility, we'll dive into the skills that'll help you shine bright and achieve your dreams. First, let's get right to the core.

Understanding Core Values

Think of your core values as your compass in life, guiding you through tough decisions and helping you stay true to yourself.

Good vs. Bad

Imagine you're at a crossroads with a choice to make: cheat on an upcoming test to guarantee a good grade or hit the books and earn that grade through hard work. This isn't just about choosing between right and wrong; it's a decision that reflects the core of who you are. Your choice in this moment is a mirror to your values —those fundamental beliefs that guide your actions and decisions every day.

Values like honesty, integrity, and fairness aren't just abstract concepts; they're the principles that anchor you in life. When you choose to study hard and earn your grade honestly, you're not just preparing for a test; you're affirming your commitment to fairness and integrity. This choice might seem harder in the moment, but these decisions build your character and shape your future self.

Understanding what's truly important to you can make all the difference in navigating life's challenges. When you're clear about your values, every decision becomes easier. You're no longer swayed by peer pressure or tempted by shortcuts because you have a strong sense of self and an inner compass that guides you toward actions you'll be proud of.

Your values do more than influence your actions; they define who you are and who you aspire to be. They shape your interactions, affect your relationships, and determine how you fit into the world around you. By staying true to your values, you ensure that you grow into the kind of person who not only achieves goals but does so in a respectful, ethical, and genuinely rewarding way.

Self-Reflection

Self-reflection is like taking a step back and looking at yourself in the mirror, but instead of seeing your physical reflection, you examine your thoughts, feelings, and actions. Regular self-reflection helps you understand your strengths and areas for improvement.

Maybe you realize you're good at listening to your friends when they need someone to talk to, but you struggle with patience when things don't go your way. Recognizing these aspects of yourself can help you grow as a person.

So, what can you do? Take some time each day to think about your actions and how they align with your values. Ask yourself questions like, "Did I treat others with kindness today?" or "Did I stand up for what I believe in?" Doing this will make you more aware of who you are and what's important to you, paving the way for personal growth and development.

Understanding your core values and practicing self-reflection are like building blocks for becoming the best version of yourself. So, take some time to think about what truly matters to you and how you can use that knowledge to navigate life's ups and downs.

Taking Ownership

You know those moments in life when things don't go as planned? Maybe you forget to complete your homework or accidentally break something at home. Well, here's the deal: You've got a choice. You can either own up to your mistakes or start pointing fingers and making excuses. How you handle these situations says a lot about the kind of person you're becoming.

Taking responsibility isn't always easy, but it's a sign of maturity. It shows that you're willing to grow and learn from your slip-ups. When you admit your faults, people respect you more because they see that you're accountable for your actions.

On the flip side, constantly making excuses and shifting blame onto others doesn't do you any favors. Sure, it might feel like you've "gotten away with it" in the moment, but it's a weak move that keeps you stuck in a cycle of dissatisfaction and victimhood.

So, think about it: Do you want to be the kind of person who owns their mistakes and grows stronger from them? Or do you want to be the type who always finds someone else to blame and ultimately lives a life of constantly feeling like a victim?

The choice is yours, but remember, it's the act of taking responsibility that ultimately separates the fulfilled and capable from the weak and frustrated.

Taking Action and Perseverance

We will discuss two super important things here: taking action and perseverance. They're like the dynamic duo of success —they work together to help you achieve your goals and dreams. To greatly simplify the concept—to make things happen in life, you only have to:

1) Start

2) Keep going until you achieve what you want.

Let's break it down.

Action

So, you've got these big dreams, right? You may want to become a professional gamer, a lion tamer, start your own business, or get into a particular college. Whatever it is, just dreaming about it won't make it happen. You've got to take action! That means putting in the work, creating a plan, and doing the things that move you closer to your goals.

Sure, it might be tempting to take shortcuts or procrastinate, but trust me, those rarely lead to success. Instead, focus on taking meaningful action daily, even if it's just a small step forward.

Perseverance

Then there's perseverance, aka *grit*. It's all about sticking with something, even when it gets tough. Look, life will throw some curveballs your way—maybe you fail a test, get rejected from your dream college, or face setbacks in your personal life. But here's the thing: setbacks aren't the end of the road; they're just detours on the path to success.

Perseverance means staying focused on your long-term goals, celebrating your progress so far, and never giving up, no matter how hard things get. Remember, every obstacle you overcome makes you stronger and brings you one step closer to your dreams.

Therefore, take the initiative, maintain concentration, and continue moving forward, even during challenging times. With determination, you can achieve anything you commit to.

When The Going Gets Tough

When you're going after something in life, you will encounter challenges. What will help you endure when the going gets tough are things like:

Patience and Flexibility

Think about it: Life is full of unexpected twists and turns. Maybe you didn't get picked for the soccer team, or your plans for the weekend fell through at the last minute. It's easy to feel frustrated or stressed out in moments like these. But that's where patience and flexibility come in handy.

Instead of getting worked up over things you can't control, try taking a deep breath and rolling with the punches. Maybe that means being patient while you work to improve your soccer skills or being flexible and finding a new way to have fun on the weekend.

Whatever the situation, practicing patience and flexibility can help you stay calm, adapt to change, and keep moving forward, even when things don't go as planned.

Adaptability

Life is inherently unpredictable, and the ability to adapt to change is crucial to maintaining both sanity and success. For instance, imagine your disappointment when your favorite band suddenly cancels their concert or your school springs a last-minute schedule change on you. While it's natural to feel upset, reacting with frustration or anger won't alter the situation. Instead, try to embrace the unexpected change and explore how you can turn it into an opportunity.

Adaptability involves more than just making the best out of a disappointing moment. It's about actively seeking out alternatives and solutions. If a concert is canceled, you could spend that evening discovering a new band or exploring other genres of music. If your school schedule changes, see it as a chance to experiment with a new routine or study method that might be more effective.

Being adaptable means being able to pivot quickly and efficiently in the face of life's twists and turns. This might involve cultivating patience, exercising flexibility, or both. These qualities are not always easy to practice consistently, but the effort is rewarding. Over time, developing these skills will make you more resilient, more open to new experiences, and more capable of overcoming challenges.

With adaptability in your toolkit, you can be confident that no matter what changes come your way, you'll handle them gracefully and emerge stronger on the other side.

Embracing Failure and Follow-Through

Failure might seem scary, but it is actually super important. Yes, you heard me right. Failure is not the end of the world. In fact, with the right mindset, it's often just a bump in the road on the way to something amazing.

Failure Is Okay

Think about it this way: Every successful person you admire has faced failure at some point. Whether it's a botched test, a missed goal in a game, or a project that didn't quite turn out as planned, failure is a natural part of life. But failure isn't a sign that you're not good enough. It's a sign that you're trying, learning, and growing.

So, instead of beating yourself up over a failure, try to see it as an opportunity to learn and improve.

Ask yourself:

- *What can I learn from this experience?*

- *How can I do better next time?*

Embracing failure is all about having the courage to try, even if there's a chance you might fall short. Because, hey, it's far better to try and fail than to never try at all.

Follow-Through

Do you know that feeling when you start something with a lot of excitement but then hit a roadblock and suddenly lose interest?

Yeah, we've all been there.

But success doesn't come from starting something—it comes from finishing it. Whether it's a project, a goal, or even just a commitment to yourself, follow-through is key. It's about sticking with something even when it gets tough, staying focused on your goals, and maintaining a positive attitude, even in the face of challenges.

So next time you feel like giving up, remember why you started in the first place. Visualize your end goal, muster up some determination, and keep pushing forward.

Keep in mind that failure doesn't mark the end of the journey—it's merely a diversion on the path to success. So, when faced with obstacles, persevere and keep moving forward.

Stop Underestimating Yourself

Have you ever been plagued by thoughts that you're not good enough, smart enough, or talented enough? These feelings can be challenging, but here's something important to remember: you are far more capable than you might believe. You *truly* have the potential to achieve extraordinary things. The key is to believe it.

Self-doubt can be a significant barrier, silently undermining your efforts and dreams. But you can combat these negative thoughts by replacing them with positive affirmations. Next time you find yourself questioning your capabilities, pause and remind yourself of your strengths.

Say it out loud:

"I am capable. I am worthy. I am unstoppable."

It's not just a mantra; **it's the truth**.

Regularly reinforcing these positive thoughts can transform how you view yourself and your abilities. Instead of being your own harshest critic, become your most supportive ally. By affirming your worth and capabilities, you'll start to see shifts not only in your self-perception but also in your actions and the outcomes you achieve.

Believing in yourself is more than an act of faith; it's a practical approach to unlocking your potential. So, embrace these affirmations and watch as you turn what seemed impossible into something perfectly achievable. Believe it.

Being Punctual

While some people think slipping into an event fashionably late is cool, it's really just another way of saying, "My time is more important than yours."

Showing up on time isn't just about not keeping others waiting—it also says a lot about your character. It shows you're reliable, responsible, and truly value others' time. Moreover, being punctual is a trait that sets you up for success across all aspects of life, from attending school to excelling in your future career, and even when you're just hanging out with friends.

So, how can you shift from "fashionably late" to 'impressively punctual'? It starts with planning.

Before your day kicks off, think about what you need to do and how much time each task will take. Set reminders on your phone—it's easy and can significantly help. Always aim to leave a little earlier than you think you should. Life is unpredictable— traffic jams happen, buses run late, and sometimes you can't find your keys. By leaving extra time for these unexpected delays, you'll arrive calm, collected, and on time.

Trust me, punctuality may seem like a minor thing, but it packs a significant punch in how others view you and your ability to meet and surpass your goals.

Once you make being on time a habit, you'll notice people will start seeing you as someone they can depend on, and doors you didn't even know existed might start opening up for you.

Cultivating Positivity

Ever noticed how negativity can spread like wildfire? It's like when one person starts complaining, suddenly everyone around them starts feeling down, too. It's as if the "Debbie Downer" zombie has bitten them, and now they're all part of the apocalyptic army of pessimism! But guess what? The same goes for positivity! When you choose to have a positive outlook, it can lift others up and create a better atmosphere for everyone.

Think of it this way: you can either be the dark rain cloud that ruins everyone's picnic, or you can be the sunshine that makes the whole day brighter. Plus, when you radiate positivity, it's like having a magnetic force field that attracts other positive people. Before you know it, you'll be surrounded by a squad of optimists ready to take on the world!

So, next time you're tempted to join in on a complaint-fest, remember that you have the power to change the narrative. Throw in a funny joke, share a silly meme, or just remind everyone of the good things in life.

Here are some quick tips for you to cultivate positivity:

Practice gratitude: Take a moment each day to think about what you're thankful for.

Surround yourself with positive influences: Spend time with friends who uplift and support you.

Focus on solutions, not problems: Instead of dwelling on what's going wrong, think about how you can make things better.

Stay active: Exercise releases endorphins, which can boost your mood.

Practice self-care: Take time to relax and do things you enjoy.

Challenge negative thoughts: Replace them with positive affirmations.

Help others: Acts of kindness can bring joy to both you and the recipient.

The Cherokee Legend Of The Two Wolves

There's a Cherokee legend about two wolves that live inside each of us. One wolf represents all the good things like kindness, love, empathy, and positivity. The other wolf embodies the negative aspects such as hate, anger, fear, and negativity. These two wolves are in a constant battle for control over our thoughts, feelings, and actions.

Now, here's the twist:

The wolf that wins *is **the one you feed***.

This powerful parable teaches us that the thoughts and emotions we focus on grow stronger within us. If we feed our minds with positive thoughts, our lives will be filled with joy, kindness, and gratitude. But if we dwell on negativity, it will consume us, leading to bitterness, resentment, and unhappiness.

This story applies to every aspect of our lives, from the way we interact with others to the goals we pursue. By consciously choosing to feed the positive wolf within us, we can cultivate a mindset of optimism, resilience, and growth. It reminds us that we have the power to shape our reality by nurturing the thoughts and emotions that serve us best.

Choosing Empathy Over Judgment

Often, we make quick judgments about others or even ourselves, which can really skew our perception. It's like wearing blinders that block out everything except one narrow perspective. However, it's vital to remember that everyone has their own unique battles and struggles. We're all striving to navigate our challenges as best we can.

So, rather than quickly judging someone based on a single action or a bad day, why not try to foster a bit more empathy? Taking just a moment to consider where someone else is coming from can dramatically change how you see them. It opens up opportunities to connect on a deeper level and build more meaningful relationships.

Remember, your attitude and the way you treat others wield significant influence. Choosing to embrace positivity and understanding can transform your interactions and create a ripple effect in your community.

Adopting this approach isn't just a minor adjustment; it's a transformative shift that can enrich your life and those of the people around you. Let's strive to see the fuller picture and spread kindness wherever we go—it's a small change that can lead to profound impacts.

Finding Your Passion

Have you ever stopped to think about what genuinely excites you? Finding your passion might seem like a daunting task, but it can be as simple as trying out new things. Step outside your comfort zone and explore a variety of hobbies, interests, and activities. This could mean joining a photography class, learning a musical instrument, experimenting with different sports, or even delving into coding or gardening. The key is to engage with a wide range of experiences until you discover something that truly lights you up.

Whether it's art, music, sports, or something entirely unexpected, follow your curiosity wherever it leads. Each new activity opens up potential passions, creating opportunities to connect with like-minded individuals and communities that share your interests. This exploration is not just about finding a pastime; it's about discovering what makes you feel most alive and connected to the world.

Once you identify something that resonates deeply with you, throw yourself into it with enthusiasm and dedication. Pursuing your passion isn't just a hobby—it can transform your life, providing a source of joy, a means of expression, and a way to achieve personal growth. It's what makes life exciting and fulfilling. So, take the leap, follow your interests, and let them evolve into passions that color your life with happiness and satisfaction. Engage fully with what you love, and watch how it expands your horizons and enriches every aspect of your existence.

Finding Balance

Life can sometimes feel like you're in the center ring of a circus, juggling multiple balls in the air—school, extracurricular activities, family, friends, and your downtime. It's like each one demands a piece of you, but the trick to keeping all the balls in the air without dropping any is finding the right balance. Just remember, if you do happen to drop a ball or two, it's not the end of the world. The key is to pick those balls back up, dust yourself off, and keep on juggling. And if all else fails, just remember: at least you're not actually in a circus. (Unless you really are, in which case, *can I get some free tickets?*)

Seriously though—finding balance means making sure no single aspect of your life overshadows the others. Achieving this balance is about more than just splitting your time evenly; it's about managing your time wisely, setting priorities based on what really matters to you, and understanding that sometimes, you need to say no.

Let's paint a picture: Imagine you've got a major exam on the horizon that could really bump up your grades. But at the same time, your friends are planning something fun that you've been looking forward to for weeks. Striking a balance doesn't mean you have to choose one over the other. Instead, you might dedicate a solid chunk of your afternoon to study, then give yourself permission to relax and enjoy hanging out with your friends afterward. This way, you're not sacrificing your social life or your academic responsibilities; you're arranging them in a way that works to your advantage.

Remember, what balance looks like can vary widely from one person to another. For some, it might mean more time with books than at basketball practice, or vice versa. The key is to experiment and figure out a routine that aligns with your goals and values and also leaves room for spontaneous fun and relaxation.

Finding your unique balance is crucial because when you get it right, life feels a lot less overwhelming and a lot more fulfilling. So, take the time to assess your priorities, listen to your needs, and adjust as necessary. That's how you keep all the balls in the air, with a smile on your face and your feet firmly on the ground.

Wrap-Up

As we conclude this chapter on personal skills, take a moment to reflect on your growth thus far. You've honed your abilities to communicate effectively, sharpened your money skills, tackled problems head-on, and even learned how to cook up a decent meal without the assistance of the fire department. Whether you realize it or not, you're making great strides toward becoming a better version of yourself, and that's a pretty special thing!

As you prepare to turn the page to the next chapter of your journey, remember that you possess the resilience and determination to overcome any obstacle. So, step forward with confidence, knowing that you have the skills and mindset to navigate whatever life throws your way.

ACTIVITY: Values Exploration

1. Grab a piece of paper and divide it into two columns.

2. In the first column, write down five values that you believe are important in life. These could be things like honesty, kindness, responsibility, respect, or creativity.

3. In the second column, write down a brief explanation of why each value is important to you. For example, if you wrote "kindness," you might explain that being kind to others makes you feel good and creates a positive environment.

4. Once you've listed your values, take a moment to reflect on how they influence your decisions and actions in your daily life.

5. Share your values and reflections with a friend or family member, discussing how they align with your goals and aspirations.

6. Challenge yourself to live according to your values each day, making choices that reflect what's truly important to you.

This activity invites you, as a teen, to delve into your core values, grasp their significance, and ponder how they shape your actions.

Chapter 7
Practical Skills

A winner is someone who recognizes his God-given talents, works his tail off to develop them into skills, and uses these skills to accomplish his goals. —Larry Bird

In this chapter, we will explore practical skills that will help you navigate life more smoothly. These skills include keeping your car in tip-top shape, dressing sharply, dealing with a traffic stop, and even sending a traditional letter.

These skills might not sound super flashy, but believe me—they're the essentials you'll be glad to have in your toolkit. So, let's get our hands dirty and dive into learning how to handle these everyday tasks like a pro. Ready? Let's do this!

Mailing a Letter

Let's tackle a skill that might seem old-fashioned but is still super relevant, even in today's modern world—mailing a letter.

You may want to send a heartfelt birthday card to a friend who lives far away, or you may need to mail some important documents for school or work. Whatever the reason, knowing how to write, address, and send a letter is a handy skill.

First off, you'll need some paper and a pen. Yeah, the old-school way! But if you're not into handwriting, typing it up on your computer is fine—whatever feels right for you. Start with what you want to say. It could be a quick "hey" to a friend or maybe a longer catch-up for someone you haven't seen in a while. Just make sure to keep it clear and include all the key points.

Once your message is down, fold your paper up neatly and pop it into an envelope. Now, for the envelope: write the recipient's full address on the front center. That includes their name, street address, city, state, and ZIP code. Pro tip: double-check the ZIP to avoid any postal mishaps.

Then, add your return address in the top left corner of the envelope. This isn't just for show —it lets the post office know where to return the letter if it can't be delivered.

When sending a letter, as long as it weighs less than 1oz, which most standard letters will, you'll only need 1 "Forever" Stamp to cover postage. Pop a stamp on the top-right corner and your letter is ready to hit the mailbox.

That's all there is to it. A simple but very practical skill.

Practical Software

You might think, "I know how to use my phone and computer; what more do I need?" But trust me, there's much more to it than just scrolling through social media.

Let's chat about essential utility software like Word, Excel, and Calendar. Microsoft Word isn't just for writing essays; it's a versatile word processor that allows you to create professional-looking documents, from school assignments to resumes and cover letters. Plus, it has handy features like spell-check and formatting options to make your writing shine.

Now, onto the Calendar app. It's not just about marking down your dentist appointments or soccer practice; it's a powerful tool for time management. You can schedule reminders for important deadlines, set recurring events for weekly activities, and even color-code your events for better organization. With your schedule at your fingertips, you'll never miss a beat.

And then there's Excel. Sure, it might seem intimidating at first, but once you get the hang of it, you'll wonder how you ever lived without it. Excel is perfect for managing budgets, tracking expenses, and creating charts and graphs to visualize data. Whether planning a budget for your next shopping spree or analyzing data for a school project, Excel is your go-to tool for crunching numbers and organizing information.

So, don't underestimate the power of these seemingly mundane software programs. They may not be as flashy as the latest social media app, but when it comes to staying organized and productive, they're indispensable. Plus, mastering these tools now will set you up for success in college, your future career, and beyond.

Public Transportation

Now, this one doesn't apply to every teen, but for those of you in a big city, knowing how to navigate public transportation opens up a world of possibilities, allowing you to explore your city and beyond. But before you set off on your journey, it's crucial to do a little homework.

Naturally, ensure that your parent or guardian is on board to allow you to travel on the buses and trains running throughout your city. They'll be able to weigh in and provide insight on whether it's a good idea to travel by yourself. That's step #1, for sure.

Start by getting familiar with the routes and schedules of buses, trains, or subways in your area. Most transit agencies have user-friendly websites or mobile apps where you can easily access this information. Take some time to explore different routes and identify the ones that will get you where you need to go.

When planning your route, there are a few key factors to consider. Think about travel time—how long will it take you to reach your destination? Look for transfer points where you may need to switch buses or trains. And, of course, prioritize safety. Pay attention to well-lit stops and busy areas, especially if you're traveling alone.

If you are unsure about a particular route or stop, feel free to ask for help. Bus drivers and transit employees are usually more than happy to assist you. Remember, it's better to ask for guidance than to get lost along the way.

Also, always have a way of communicating with your home base while traveling on public transport. It's good practice to let them know where you're going and when you plan to arrive just so they can keep tabs on you and help ensure safe travels.

Stay in School

This one's a big deal: Finishing school is like building the ultimate foundation for whatever extraordinary future you've got in mind. There are days when school feels like a total slog—homework piles up, exams loom, and some lessons feel like they'll never end. But hang in there because every task you tackle is an investment in your future.

Now, don't get the wrong idea—I'm not saying it's all going to be a breeze. School is definitely going to toss some challenges your way. Maybe it's a brutal math assignment, a super strict teacher, or your own personal stuff that gets in the way. But guess what? During these challenging times, you really find out what you're made of. You learn a ton, not just about subjects, but about yourself too.

And hey, if the pressure ever gets too much, there's no shame in reaching out for some help. Whether it's confusion over a calculus problem or something personal getting you down, there's always someone around who's ready to help. Remember, asking for help isn't a sign of weakness—it shows you've got the guts to tackle your challenges head-on.

So keep at it, and don't be afraid to lean on others when necessary. School's not just about grades and graduation—it's a journey of growing into who you're meant to be.

Reading a Map

In today's digital age, GPS has become a go-to for navigation, but what if you're in a situation without a signal or battery? That's where map-reading skills step in.

Start by getting comfortable with the symbols and legends on the map. Landmarks are your friends. Use them to figure out where you are. Street names, intersections, and distance scales are crucial for accurately plotting your route. Oh, and don't overlook things like terrain and elevation changes. They can throw you off if you're not careful.

The more you practice reading maps, the better you'll get. Take every opportunity to hone your skills. Whether you're on a road trip, hiking in the great outdoors, or just wandering around your neighborhood. Not only will it sharpen your navigation abilities, but it'll also give you a sense of empowerment and self-sufficiency.

So, when your phone's GPS decides to take a break, you'll lead the way confidently, navigating like a seasoned explorer!

Dress for Success

Your appearance can make a big impression, whether you're heading to a job interview, meeting new people, or just going about your day. Dressing neatly and appropriately shows that you take pride in yourself and respect the situation you're in (and no, your favorite jammies don't count as "appropriate" for most occasions, no matter how comfy they are).

For boys, this might mean wearing clean, well-fitted clothes like a button-down shirt, trousers, and dress shoes for more formal occasions or a polo shirt and jeans for a casual look. Girls can opt for a blouse or dress paired with flats or heels for a polished appearance or a nice top and skirt for a more relaxed vibe.

Remember, dressing for success isn't about wearing expensive designer labels—it's about choosing clothes that fit well, are clean and wrinkle-free, and make you feel confident and comfortable. So, whether you're dressing up for a special event or just want to make a good impression, put your best foot forward and show the world what you're made of.

Know Your Rights

As a teen, it's essential to be aware of your fundamental rights. While these may vary slightly depending on where you live, here are some basic rights that every teen should know:

- **The right to education:** You have the right to access free, quality education that helps you develop your talents and abilities.
- **Freedom of expression:** You have the right to express your opinions, ideas, and beliefs as long as they don't infringe on the rights of others or promote hate or violence.
- **Privacy:** You have the right to privacy, which means you can control who has access to your personal information, both online and offline.
- **Protection from abuse and neglect:** You have the right to be safe from physical, emotional, and sexual abuse, as well as neglect.
- **Health care:** You have the right to access quality health care services, including mental health support.
- **Fair labor practices:** If you work, you have the right to fair wages, safe working conditions, and reasonable hours.
- **Equal treatment:** You have the right to be treated equally regardless of your race, gender, religion, sexual orientation, or disability.
- **Due process:** If you're accused of a crime, you have the right to a fair trial and legal representation.
- **Freedom of association:** You have the right to join clubs, organizations, or groups that align with your interests and beliefs.
- **Participation in decisions that affect you:** You have the right to have a say in decisions that impact your life, such as your education or health care.

Remember, knowing your rights is the first step in advocating for yourself and others. If you ever feel like your rights are being violated, don't hesitate to reach out to a trusted adult for help and guidance.

Learning to Drive

Learning to drive is a rite of passage that opens up a world of freedom and independence, and also the ability to impress your friends with your parallel parking skills. Still, it's also a responsibility that shouldn't be taken lightly. You don't want to be that person who thinks turn signals are optional and speed limits are just friendly suggestions. Beyond just understanding how to operate a vehicle, it's about developing the mindset and habits of a responsible driver who prioritizes safety.

Think of driving like a group project—everyone has to do their part to make it a success. It means always being aware of your surroundings, even if you're jamming out to your favorite tunes. It means following traffic laws, even when you're pretty sure you could totally beat that yellow light. And it means making intelligent decisions, like not texting while driving, no matter how hilarious that meme your bestie sent you seems.

So, when you're gearing up to hit the road, start by familiarizing yourself with the basics. Adjusting your mirrors, signaling properly, and obeying traffic laws seem like small details, but they're absolutely the building blocks of safe driving habits. And don't hesitate to ask questions or seek guidance from a trusted adult who can share their wisdom and experience with you.

Of course, practice is key to mastering any skill, and driving is no exception. Don't be afraid to log those hours behind the wheel, whether in an empty parking lot, on quiet neighborhood streets, or even on the highway with a seasoned driver by your side. Each experience behind the wheel will help build your confidence and competence as a driver.

But remember, safety always comes first. Buckle up, put away distractions like your phone, and always stay focused on the road ahead. Don't forget to watch for other drivers, pedestrians, and potential hazards. Defensive driving is a crucial skill that can help you avoid accidents and stay safe on the road.

Changing A Flat Tire

Imagine you're cruising down the road with your favorite tunes playing, and suddenly, you hear that dreaded flub-flub-flub sound. Yep, you've got a flat tire.

But no sweat. Changing a tire is a fundamental skill you can totally master, and it's your ticket to not being stranded on the side of the road.

Here's how to perform a tire change like a pro:

1. Safety First: Before doing anything, ensure you're parked safely away from traffic and on level ground. Turn on your hazard lights to alert other drivers, and if you have them, place reflective cones or triangles behind your vehicle.

2. Prep Your Tools: Pop the trunk and grab your spare tire, jack, and lug wrench. These are your new best friends. Make sure the spare tire is inflated and in good shape.

3. Loosen the Lug Nuts: Before you jack up the car, use the lug wrench to loosen the lug nuts on the flat tire. Turn them counterclockwise just enough to break their resistance. You'll completely remove them later, but it's easier to start when the tire is still on the ground, so it doesn't spin.

4. Lift the Car: Slide the jack under the car along the frame near the flat tire (your car's manual will show you the exact spot). Crank the jack to lift the tire off the ground. You need enough height to remove the flat and fit the spare.

5. Swap the Tire: Remove the loosened lug nuts and pull the tire off the hub. Slide the spare onto the hub, line up the holes, and screw the lug nuts on by hand. Then, snug them up with the wrench while the car is still lifted.

6. Lower and Tighten: Lower the car back to the ground. Give those lug nuts one last tighten, this time using your full strength to ensure they're super tight.

7. Pack Up: Put the flat tire and all your tools back in your trunk. Don't forget to turn off your hazards!

Congrats! You've just changed your tire and saved the day. Remember, this is a temporary fix —get that flat properly repaired or replaced ASAP to keep your chariot in prime condition.

DIY Car Maintenance

Think of DIY car care as giving your ride a little TLC. It's not just about keeping it looking good; it's about extending your four-wheeled friend's life, safety, and performance. Let's break it down into a few essential tasks that'll keep your car happy.

Wash Your Car Regularly: Getting out the hose, bucket, and soap isn't just about vanity—washing your car can protect its paint from dirt, grime, and rust, all of which can cause long-term damage if left unchecked. Plus, there's nothing quite like the feeling of cruising around in a car that shines like new.

Change Your Wiper Blades: Imagine driving in heavy rain, and your wipers are smudging water across the windshield. Not fun, right? Old, worn-out wiper blades can make driving in bad weather dangerous. Replacing them is simple, cost-effective, and ensures you can see clearly, regardless of weather. This small step can be a literal lifesaver.

Check and Change Your Oil: Keeping an eye on your oil level and color is crucial for your engine's health. Pull out the dipstick, wipe it clean, dip it back in, pull it back out again, and check where the oil sits. It should be within the marked areas and look relatively clean. Old or dirty oil can cause serious engine problems. Most car experts recommend changing your oil every 3000 miles or as specified in your owner's manual. Regular oil changes keep your engine running smoothly and can prevent costly repairs down the line.

Monitor Your Tire Pressure: Low tire pressure can lead to poor fuel economy, faster tire wear, and reduced safety. It's super easy to check: just use a tire pressure gauge on each tire, including the spare. Make sure the pressure matches the PSI recommended in your car's manual. Adjust as necessary using an air pump at most gas stations.

By managing these core aspects of car maintenance, you're not just caring for your car; you're ensuring a safer, smoother ride. Plus, getting hands-on with your vehicle is empowering. It builds confidence and knowledge, which are just as important on the road as a full gas tank. So, roll up your sleeves and take charge next time your car needs a little care. Your car (and your wallet) will thank you.

How To Act During A Traffic Stop

Picture this: you're cruising down the highway, singing along to your favorite song *(waaay off-key, but who's listening?)*, when suddenly, you see those infamous flashing red and blue lights in your rearview mirror. Your heart sinks as you realize you're being pulled over.

Now, before you panic and start crafting an elaborate story about how you were rushing to save a litter of kittens from a burning building, let's talk about how to handle this.

First, don't even think about pulling a fast one and trying to outrun the cops. This isn't a video game, and you're not invincible. Plus, let's be real, your mom's minivan isn't exactly built for high-speed chases. Instead, slow down, put on your turn signal, and carefully pull over to the right side of the road.

Once you've stopped, take a deep breath and remember that the officer is just doing their job. They're not out to get you (unless you've been driving like a maniac, in which case, you might want to rethink your life choices). Turn off the engine, roll down your window, and keep your hands visible on the steering wheel. No sudden movements, no reaching for your phone to live-tweet the experience, and definitely no sassy comebacks.

When the officer approaches, be polite and respectful. Address them as "Officer" and answer their questions honestly (but remember, you have the right to remain silent if you're unsure about something). If they ask for your license and registration, let them know where you're reaching before you do it. And if you do end up with a ticket, resist the urge to argue or make a scene. Save that energy for telling the story to your friends later (with a few embellishments, of course).

So, there you have it - the dos and don'ts of surviving a traffic stop. Just remember, a little bit of respect and common sense can go a long way in keeping the situation calm and drama-free. And who knows, if you play your cards right, you might even get off with a warning (but don't count on it, lead foot).

Voting

This one's specifically for those who are 18 and up, but stick around even if you're younger. This is important to understand because voting is your golden ticket to influencing the future.

You've probably seen loads of stuff about voting during significant elections, like when we're choosing the next president. But here's the scoop: voting is about much more than deciding who gets to sit in the Oval Office. It's your chance to weigh in on the decisions that shape your community, state, country, and even the world.

So, why should you care? Think of voting as the most direct way to make your voice heard in the government. It's how you get a say in what happens around you, from policies on education and healthcare to decisions on public transportation and environmental protection. Every single vote contributes to the outcome, shaping not just the present but the future as well.

So when you finally hit that age where you can cast your ballot, remember: your vote isn't just a right; it's a powerful tool to help steer our country in the direction you believe it should go. Don't let it go to waste. Even if you're under 18, get ready, get informed, and get excited. Your time to vote will come; when it does, you'll be prepared to make a difference. Your vote is your voice. It matters more than you think.

ACTIVITY: Perform An Oil Check

Learn how to properly check the oil level in a car under adult supervision and understand its importance for vehicle maintenance.

- With an adult's assistance, park the car on a level surface and turn off the engine. Let the car sit for 5-10 minutes to allow the oil to settle.
- Open the hood and locate the oil dipstick (consult the owner's manual if needed).
- Pull out the dipstick and wipe it clean with the rag or paper towel.
- Reinsert the dipstick fully, then pull it out again.
- Check the oil level on the dipstick. The oil should be between the minimum and maximum marks.
- If the oil level is low, consult with the adult to add the recommended oil gradually (as specified in the owner's manual) and recheck the level.
- If the oil level is above the maximum mark (this is seldom the case), some oil may need to be drained or there could be a larger issue. Ask the adult to help you consult a professional mechanic in this case.
- Reinsert the dipstick and close the hood.

Make it a habit to check your car's oil level at least once a month or before long trips to ensure your engine stays properly lubricated and to catch any potential issues early.

Chapter 8
The Skill Of Altruism

Being altruistic often consists of nothing more than extending a hand to someone in need —Anonymous

Ever heard of **altruism**? It's like being a *secret superhero*, but instead of wearing a cape, you're armed with kindness and a willingness to help others just because it's the right thing

to do.

To better understand, here's a question for you to ponder:

Would you be willing to help someone you've never met, even if they'll never know it was you who helped them?

Who is this mystery person? Well, they're a bit like how you used to be. They're searching for answers to make their journey through life a little easier, but they don't know exactly where to look.

I believe this book can help them, *but how can they find it?* That's where your Skill Of Altruism comes in!

You see, many people decide which book to read based on what others think about it. That's why I'm asking for your help on behalf of many teens you've never met:

Please take a moment to leave a review for this book.

It doesn't cost a dime and will only take about a minute of your time, yet it can significantly impact the lives of other teens like you.

Your review could help:

- One more young person feel understood and supported.
- One more teenager navigate challenges with confidence.
- One more student improve their decision-making.
- One more future leader discover their potential.
- One more dreamer believe in their dreams.

To get that "feel good" feeling and really make a difference, all it takes is less than a minute to:

Leave a review.

Just scan the QR code below to share your thoughts:

If the idea of helping out a young stranger you'll never meet makes you smile, then you have an altruistic heart, and that's a beautiful thing.

Thank you for leaving a review. Your biggest fan,

~ Ben Clardy

Now, let's get back to it!

Chapter 9

Productivity Skills

The secret of getting ahead is getting started.
—Mark Twain

Ever feel like you've got a mountain of tasks staring you down, but you're not sure where to start? Sometimes, taking that first step is the hardest part, but once you do, you'll be amazed at what you can accomplish. Throughout this chapter, we'll explore practical strategies to help you manage your time effectively, stay focused on your goals, and tackle tasks with confidence.

Understanding Procrastination

Procrastination is the tendency to delay or postpone tasks, especially important ones, in favor of more pleasurable activities. It's like having a little devil on your shoulder, whispering sweet nothings about how much more fun it would be to watch cat videos or scroll through memes instead of tackling that essay or studying for that exam. Procrastination often stems from factors like fear of failure, lack of motivation, or feeling overwhelmed by the task at hand.

Procrastination is like the junk food of productivity—it feels good in the moment, but it doesn't do you any favors in the long run. And just like with junk food, the more you indulge in procrastination, the harder it becomes to break the habit.

So, how do you kick procrastination to the curb? Well, it starts with recognizing the problem and understanding why you're tempted to put things off in the first place. Is it because the task seems too daunting? Break it down into smaller, more manageable steps. Is it because you're not sure where to start? Try the "two-minute rule"—commit to working on the task for just two minutes, and chances are, you'll find yourself getting into a groove.

And remember, it's okay to take breaks and reward yourself for making progress. Just make sure your rewards don't turn into full-blown procrastination sessions (because that "quick" YouTube break can easily turn into a three-hour rabbit hole of rabbit videos because... I've been there).

Breaking the Habit

Want to kick an old habit to the curb and start fresh? Whether it's procrastinating on homework, spending too much time on your phone, or anything else you want to change, developing new habits is key. Here's how you can get organized and make your new habits stick. By following these steps, you'll build a routine that works for you, keeps you focused, and makes your goals achievable. Let's break it down:

- **Set clear goals:** Break tasks into smaller, manageable steps and set deadlines for each.

- **Create a schedule:** Utilize a planner or digital calendar to schedule dedicated time slots for each task.

- **Eliminate distractions:** Identify common distractions like social media, video games, or TV, and limit your exposure to them during work or study sessions.

- **Practice self-discipline:** Hold yourself accountable for sticking to your schedule and completing tasks on time.

- **Reward yourself:** Celebrate small victories along the way to reinforce positive behaviors and motivate yourself to keep going.

Benefits of Taking Action

Ever feel like you're stuck in a cycle of procrastination, stress, and last-minute panic? Breaking out of that loop starts with a straightforward step: *taking action.* When you start completing tasks proactively, you're not just ticking boxes—you're setting yourself up for a whole host of benefits. Here's what you can expect when you take charge and get ahead of your to-dos:

- **Reduced stress:** Completing tasks ahead of time eliminates the pressure of looming deadlines.

- Increased productivity: Promptly tackling tasks frees up time for other activities and prevents the accumulation of unfinished work.

- Improved self-confidence: Accomplishing goals boosts self-esteem and provides a sense of accomplishment.

Common Distractions for Teens

In today's digital age, distractions are just a click away, especially for teens who are trying to balance schoolwork, hobbies, and social life. These interruptions can make it difficult to focus and stay on task. Understanding what typically distracts you is the first step toward managing your time better and boosting your productivity. Here are some of the most common culprits that might be pulling your attention away:

- Social media: Constant notifications from apps like Instagram, Snapchat, and TikTok can disrupt focus.

- Video games: Engaging gameplay and multiplayer features can make it challenging to tear away from the screen.

- Smartphones: Text messages, calls, and browsing the web can lure attention away from more important tasks.

Strategies to Minimize Distraction

With a few intentional strategies, you can significantly reduce these interruptions and enhance your ability to concentrate on what truly matters. Whether it's homework, studying, or personal projects, applying effective methods to minimize distractions can make a substantial difference. Here are some practical strategies that can help you stay on track and maintain your focus:

- Set boundaries: Establish designated times for using social media and playing video games to avoid constant interruptions.

- Use productivity apps: Install apps or browser extensions that block distracting websites or limit screen time.

- Create a distraction-free environment: Designate a quiet, clutter-free workspace where you can concentrate without disruptions.

- Practice mindfulness: Stay present and focused on the task at hand, resisting the urge to multitask or switch between activities.

Knockout The Homework

Homework might not top your list of fun activities, but it's a key player in your academic journey. Yes, diving into assignments after a full day of school might seem like a drag, but think of homework as the secret sauce that boosts your understanding and retention of classroom material.

Now, let's talk strategy. Knocking out your homework early doesn't just free up your evenings—it also slashes stress and anxiety right out of your daily routine. Break down those big, scary projects into smaller, bite-sized tasks. This approach keeps you from feeling overwhelmed and helps you tackle each part with clear focus and determination.

And here's the real win: Finishing your homework ahead of time isn't just about getting it done—it's about setting yourself up for future triumphs. With your assignments out of the way, you've got extra time to dive into hobbies, hang out with friends, or just chill and recharge.

In the long run, managing your homework efficiently doesn't just boost your grades. It creates more space in your life for growth, relaxation, and exploration.

Prioritizing Tasks

Prioritizing tasks is all about knowing what needs to be done first and why. You might have a list of things to do, but not all of them are equally urgent or important. Here's how to tell the difference.

Weighing Importance & Urgency

You're hanging out and having fun, and suddenly, your phone lights up with a text message. This message demands your immediate attention, making it feel urgent, but there's a catch. The content of that message, usually a meme, a funny video, or a simple greeting—isn't actually important, especially not in the grand scheme of things. It feels urgent because it's immediate, but it lacks significant long-term impact.

Next, consider this scenario: You're preparing for an important presentation at school that counts significantly towards your final grade. It's scheduled for first thing tomorrow morning. Just as you're about to go to bed, you realize you've left your USB drive with the presentation files at a friend's house across town. This situation becomes truly urgent because retrieving the drive is essential for your presentation. Immediate action is required to ensure you have everything you need to avoid a significant impact on your grade. If you don't act quickly, you risk going unprepared and potentially facing significant negative consequences.

The next time you're interrupted by something that seems urgent, pause and ask yourself, "Is this as important as the other tasks I have?" If the answer is no, give yourself permission to postpone it.

By focusing on what's truly important, you're not only setting yourself up for success now but also developing essential prioritization skills that will serve you well throughout life.

Setting Daily Priorities

You're bombarded with things to do every day. It can be challenging to know when to do what, especially when everything seems to be screaming, *"Pick me! Pick me!"* like an overeager kid in class. Setting daily priorities helps you focus on what really matters and prevents you from feeling overwhelmed.

When you set daily priorities, you're not just randomly picking tasks to focus on like you're playing a game of "eeny, meeny, miny, moe." You're intentionally choosing the things that will move you closer to your goals or help you handle pressing responsibilities.

And remember, it's okay if your priorities shift throughout the day. Life has a way of throwing curveballs (like a surprise math quiz or a last-minute project), and sometimes you need to adjust your plan. The key is to stay flexible and keep your eye on the prize. With a bit of practice and a lot of determination, you'll be a daily priority-setting pro in no time!

Identifying Top Priorities

Identifying your top priorities means figuring out what tasks are the most important for you to accomplish each day. These are the things that absolutely need your attention and effort. For example, if you have a big project due at school or an important exam coming up, those would likely be your top priorities. Think about what tasks will have the most significant impact on your day or move you closer to your goals. By focusing on these top priorities, you can make sure you're using your time and energy in the most effective way possible.

Focusing on Daily Goals

Alright, now that you know your top priorities for the day, let's zoom in a bit and talk about focusing on your daily goals. Think of it as setting mini-milestones for yourself—little checkpoints that keep you moving forward.

So, let's say you've got a research paper broken down into sections. Each day, set a goal to tackle one or two of those sections. Maybe today, you'll knock out the introduction and outline the body paragraphs. Tomorrow, you'll dive into the research for those paragraphs and so on.

By setting these daily goals, you're giving yourself a clear roadmap for what you want to achieve each day. It's like having a little to-do list within your more enormous to-do list. Plus, crossing off those daily goals feels seriously satisfying. It's like a little victory dance every time you check something off. And before you know it, all those daily wins add up to some significant progress on your bigger tasks.

A Cool Trick For Prioritization

One way to sort and prioritize tasks visually is to use an "Eisenhower Box."

It looks like this:

	Urgent	Not Urgent
Important	**Do**	**Decide**
Not Important	**Delegate**	**Delete**

The thing about the Eisenhower Box is that it's designed to be used mentally, but for the sake of clarity, here's how it works visually:

In the upper/left box, you've got tasks that are both important and urgent, like if you have a deadline coming up or a sudden problem to solve.

The upper/right box is where tasks are important but not super urgent. This could be stuff like planning for a project or studying for a test that's still a few days away.

In the lower/left box is where you place tasks that are urgent but not that important. Think of things that pop up and demand your attention, like responding to non-urgent emails.

Finally, you've got the lower/right box, which is where you put tasks that are neither urgent nor important, like binge-watching a show.

By putting your tasks into these boxes, you get a clearer picture of what needs your immediate attention and what can wait. It's like having a roadmap for your day, helping you focus on what really matters and avoid getting sidetracked by less important stuff. So, give it a try next time you're feeling overwhelmed and need some help prioritizing things.

The Art Of "Saying No"

I know it might feel like you have to be a hero and save the day for everyone, but trust me, even superheroes need a break sometimes. Saying "no" doesn't make you selfish or lazy—it means you're taking care of yourself and your well-being.

Imagine this: you're already swamped with schoolwork, extracurriculars, and maybe even a part-time job. Then, out of the blue, someone asks you to help organize a fundraiser or join a new club. Before you jump in headfirst, take a moment to think about whether you can handle it without sacrificing your sanity. If the answer is no, don't be afraid to decline politely. It's better to do a few things well than to spread yourself too thin and end up feeling overwhelmed.

But let's say you do decide to take on a new challenge. Maybe it's something you're really passionate about or an opportunity to learn and grow. That's awesome! Just make sure it aligns with your priorities and goals. Will it help you reach your long-term objectives, or will it just add more stress to your plate? Be honest with yourself and choose wisely.

Rewarding Progress

Who doesn't love a little treat for crushing their goals, right? Let's say you've just finished a marathon study session without falling asleep on your textbook, aced that test, or completed a daunting assignment that was so long that you thought you might need a passport to reach the end. Now, it's time to celebrate your hard work!

Think about what gets you excited. Maybe it's a slice of your favorite pizza? Or perhaps a scoop of ice cream or two, or three – I won't judge. It could even be just a few minutes of scrolling guilt-free and enjoying some hilarious cat videos. Whatever it is, make it something that makes you smile and gives you a little pick-me-up!

And here's the best part: rewards aren't just about indulging in the moment, although that's definitely a bonus. They're also about giving yourself something to look forward to as you tackle your to-do list. Knowing that there's a yummy snack or a mini Netflix break waiting for you at the end can be seriously motivating. It's like having a little cheerleader in your brain, urging you on with pom-poms and promises of deliciousness.

So don't be afraid to treat yourself—you've earned it, champ! Just remember, moderation is key. Now go forth, conquer that homework, and enjoy your well-deserved reward.

Harnessing Habits For Productivity

Did you know that your habits can either make or break your productivity game? It's true! By establishing positive habits, you can automate certain behaviors and make getting stuff done feel like second nature.

For example, if you make it a habit to review your to-do list every morning or spend 10 minutes tidying up your workspace at the end of each day, you'll end up with a cleaner, more organized life.

Pretty self-explanatory, right?

Plus, once those habits are ingrained, you'll find yourself crushing tasks left and right without even thinking about it.

Creating Morning and Evening Routines

Alright, let's paint a picture here...

You open your eyes in the morning, feeling like you've just had the best sleep of your life. What's next? Maybe you start with a quick stretch, reaching for the sky and wiggling your toes to wake up your body. Then, it's time for breakfast—a hearty bowl of oatmeal topped with your favorite fruits, perhaps, or a smoothie packed with energy-boosting ingredients. While you munch away, you take a peek at your schedule for the day. What classes do you have? Any important deadlines or appointments? By checking in with your schedule first thing, you set yourself up for success and avoid any last-minute surprises.

Now, let's fast forward to the end of the day. You've conquered your classes, aced that test, and crushed your extracurricular activities. Now it's time to wind down and relax. Maybe you curl up with a good book. A thrilling mystery or an epic fantasy adventure. As you lose yourself in the pages, you feel the stress of the day melting away. Or perhaps you prefer to jot down any thoughts or tasks swirling around in your head in your trusty journal. By getting everything down on paper, you clear your mind and make space for a peaceful night's sleep. And hey, why not take a few minutes to pick out tomorrow's outfit? That way, you can hit the ground running when morning comes.

So there you have it. A morning and evening routine fit for a teen on a mission to conquer the world (or at least their homework). With a little structure and a whole lot of intention, you'll be well on your way to starting and ending each day on the right foot.

Adjusting Routines Over Time

Now, here's the thing about routines—they're not set in stone. As you grow and your priorities change, it's important to adjust your routines accordingly.

Maybe you used to be a night owl, but now you're more productive in the morning. Or perhaps you've discovered a new hobby that you want to make time for in your evening routine. Whatever it is, don't be afraid to tweak your routines to suit your evolving needs and goals.

Utilizing Task Management Apps

Task management apps can be a game-changer when it comes to staying organized and on top of your to-do list. Whether you prefer a simple checklist-style app or something more robust with features like deadlines, reminders, and categorization, there's a task management app out there for you.

First up, we've got Todoist. It's super user-friendly and perfect if you like to keep things simple with a basic checklist. Just pop in your tasks, set deadlines, and you're good to go. Plus, it syncs across all your devices, so you can stay on top of things no matter where you are.

If you're looking for something a bit more advanced, Trello might be right up your alley. It's like having a virtual bulletin board where you can organize your tasks into different boards and lists. You can add due dates, attach files, and even collaborate with friends on group projects. Talk about teamwork!

And, of course, let's not forget about calendars and scheduling tools. Digital calendars are a great way to keep track of appointments, deadlines, and important events. Whether you use Google Calendar, Apple Calendar, or another digital calendar app, having all your commitments laid out in one place can help you stay organized and ensure that nothing slips through the cracks.

Last but not least, let's talk about note-taking and idea-capture apps. Whether you're jotting down notes in class, brainstorming ideas for a project, or just need a place to keep track of random thoughts, having a reliable note-taking app on your phone or computer can be a lifesaver.

Apps like Evernote, OneNote, Notability, or even just the Notes app on your smartphone make it easy to capture ideas on the go and access them whenever you need them.

Goal Setting and Progress Tracking

Setting goals and tracking progress are pivotal for personal and professional growth. Together, these practices empower you to steer confidently toward your desired outcomes and manage your journey effectively.

Setting Long-Term vs. Short-Term Goals

Long-term goals are the big-ticket dreams that light up your future, kind of like the ultimate destinations on your personal road map. Maybe you see yourself tossing your graduation cap in the air, kicking off a killer career, or backpacking across Europe. These aren't just any goals; they're your hopes and aspirations that pull you forward through life's ups and downs.

On the flip side, short-term goals are like the signposts along the way. They're the manageable, bite-sized tasks that pave your path toward those big dreams. Think about taking that algebra test next week or saving a chunk of your weekend job earnings for a new laptop. These goals might seem small in comparison, but they're crucial. They keep you moving forward, one step at a time, and give you quick wins that boost your confidence and motivation.

Together, long-term and short-term goals work hand in hand. While your long-term goals give you a vision to strive for, your short-term goals offer daily or weekly focuses that make the big dreams feel achievable. They provide structure and momentum in your daily life, helping you stay on track and pushing you towards those bigger aspirations.

Understanding the difference between long-term and short-term goals and how they work together is the key to not just dreaming about the future you want but *actually making it happen.*

Visualizing Goals

Imagine yourself taking that big exam, landing that dream internship, or finally mastering that killer dance routine. What do you see? Are you celebrating with friends and family? High-fiving your future self? Take a mental snapshot of that moment and hold onto it tight.

Now, let's get practical. Break down that big, beautiful vision into bite-sized pieces. Maybe you create a vision board filled with inspiring images and quotes, or you jot down your goals in a journal every morning. Heck, you could even make a Pinterest board dedicated to your dreams. Who says goal-setting can't be stylish?

The key is to make it fun and personal. Find whatever gets your creative juices flowing—whether it's doodling in a notebook, creating a digital collage, or blasting your favorite tunes while you brainstorm. Remember, this is your dream world, so paint it however you like!

Monitoring Progress and Adjusting Goals

Checking in on your progress is like checking the map on a road trip. It helps you see if you're on track or if you need to make a U-turn. So, whip out your favorite method for keeping tabs on your goals. Whether it's ticking tasks off a checklist, updating a progress bar in an app, or scribbling in a journal, find what works for you and stick with it.

Now, here's the best part—adjusting your goals. If you find that your original plan isn't quite hitting the spot, don't sweat it! Take a step back, reassess the situation, and be open to trying a new approach. Maybe you need to break a big goal into smaller chunks, switch up your tactics, or even set a new goal altogether.

Remember, flexibility is your bestie on this journey, so don't be afraid to shake things up if you need to. The important thing is to keep moving forward, even if the path takes a few unexpected twists and turns.

ACTIVITY: Goal-Setting Challenge

Step 1: Set aside some quiet time to reflect on your goals, both short and long-term. Write them down in a journal or on your phone.

Step 2: Divide your objectives into more achievable tasks. Consider the necessary actions to progress towards each goal. Remember the part about long-term & short-term goals? This is it in action.

Step 3: Create a visual representation of your goals, like a vision board or a digital collage. Use pictures, quotes, and symbols that inspire you.

Step 4: Discuss your goals with a friend or family member. Sharing your goals can keep you responsible and driven.

Keep in mind that each step you take, regardless of its size, propels you nearer to your aspirations. Therefore, continue establishing goals, making steady progress, and persistently reaching for the stars.

Chapter 10

Social Skills

Your smile is your logo. Your personality is your business card. How you leave others feeling after having an experience with you becomes your trademark.
—Jay Danzie

In this chapter, we'll unpack the art of communication, the magic of making friends, and the finesse of handling tricky situations with grace. So buckle up, buttercup, and get ready to learn some life-changing skills that will help you become a master of your social world.

Social Etiquette and Manners

Social interactions can be a breeze when you know the ropes of etiquette and manners. It's all about treating others with courtesy and respect, which means being kind, considerate, and mindful of other people's feelings. Think about it— would you want someone to interrupt you while you're speaking or ignore you when you're trying to join a conversation? Of course not! So, be sure to listen actively, wait your turn to speak, and show genuine interest in what others have to say.

When you're at the table, remember to keep your elbows off it, chew with your mouth closed, and use your utensils like a pro. And if you're using your phone during a meal, try to keep it discreet—nobody likes feeling ignored or sidelined by someone scrolling through Instagram mid-conversation.

When it comes to socializing, a few simple tips can make a big difference. Remember to smile, establish eye contact, and extend a firm handshake when encountering someone for the first time. And don't forget the power of a genuine compliment or a simple "thank you"—it can greatly make others feel appreciated and valued.

So, whether you're at a party, a family gathering, or just hanging out with friends, remember to bring your A-game in manners and etiquette—it's the key to making lasting connections and leaving a positive impression wherever you go.

Social Radar

Personal protection is not just about physical safety, although that's important too. It's also about protecting yourself from situations and relationships that just aren't good for you. So, how do you do that? Well, it starts with recognizing the warning signs.

Think about it like this: Have you ever been in a social situation where something didn't feel right? Maybe you felt uncomfortable, pressured, or like something was off. Those are all warning signs that something might not be entirely kosher. Whether it's a sketchy party, a toxic friendship, or a relationship going south, it's crucial to trust your gut and make decisions prioritizing your well-being.

And speaking of decisions, let's focus on that for a second. Sometimes, it can be tempting to go along with the crowd or ignore our instincts to avoid conflict. But here's the thing: your safety and happiness are worth standing up for. Don't be afraid to assert yourself and say no when something doesn't feel right. Whether setting boundaries with friends, saying no to peer pressure, or walking away from a toxic relationship, remember that you have the power to protect yourself.

Being assertive doesn't mean being rude or aggressive. You just have to be confident, respectful, and firm in your decisions. And hey, it's okay to ask for help if you need it. Whether it's talking to a trusted adult, seeking guidance from a counselor, or reaching out to a hotline, there are people who care about you and want to support you.

Relationships

Friendships and relationships can be incredible, but they can also go bad sometimes. Unhealthy relationships can come in many forms, from friendships to romantic connections. Here are some signs to watch out for:

- Lack of Respect: If someone consistently disregards your feelings, boundaries, or opinions, it's a red flag. Respect should be mutual in any relationship.

- Constant Criticism: Constructive feedback is one thing, but constant criticism that makes you feel small or inadequate is another. Healthy relationships involve support and encouragement, not tearing each other down.

- Control Issues: Whether it's trying to control what you wear, who you spend time with, or how you behave, control issues can be a sign of an unhealthy dynamic.

- Unbalanced Power: In healthy relationships, power is shared, and decisions are made together. If one person always holds the upper hand or manipulates situations to their advantage, it's a warning sign.

- Lack of Trust: Trust is the foundation of any healthy relationship. If you constantly feel distrustful or betrayed, it's a sign that something isn't right.

Remember, it's OK to walk away from relationships that don't make you feel valued or respected.

Healthy Boundaries

Picture this: you're getting to know someone, and everything initially seems great. But as time passes, you start to notice little things that don't sit right with you. Maybe they're constantly monitoring you, invading your personal space, or pressuring you to do things you're uncomfortable with. That's where setting boundaries comes into play.

First, it's important to know what you're comfortable with and what you're not. Maybe you're okay with holding hands but not ready for anything more, or perhaps you need some alone time to focus on school or hobbies. Whatever it is, trust your instincts and communicate your boundaries respectfully.

When it comes to setting boundaries, honesty is key. It's okay to speak up and let the other person know how you're feeling. You might say something like, "Hey, I really enjoy spending time with you, but I need some space to focus on my studies right now." Remember, it's not about blaming or accusing—it's about respectfully expressing your needs and expectations.

Maintaining your personal health and well-being should always be a top priority. If someone makes you uncomfortable or doesn't respect your boundaries, it's okay to walk away. You deserve to be around people who respect you and treat you with kindness and understanding.

Dating Dynamics

Look, crushes and feelings are totally normal, but remember, there's no rush to dive headfirst into a relationship. Take your time, get to know the person, and most importantly, prioritize your safety and well-being.

When it comes to dating, safety should always be a top priority. Whether you're meeting someone new or going on a date with someone you know, let a friend or family member know where you'll be and who you'll be with. And trust your instincts. If something doesn't feel right, don't hesitate to speak up or remove yourself from the situation.

Now, let's move on to setting paces and making sound decisions. There's no rulebook for dating, and everyone moves at their own pace. Whether you're ready to take things slow or jump right in, it's important to communicate openly and honestly with your date about your boundaries and expectations. And remember, consent is key. Always ask for and respect your partner's boundaries.

If you ever find yourself in a situation where you're feeling pressured or uncomfortable, it's absolutely okay to say "no." Your priority should always be your own well-being, and a strong relationship is founded on mutual respect and empathy.

So, whether you're navigating your first crush or embarking on a new relationship, remember to prioritize safety, communicate openly, and trust your instincts. Dating should be a fun and exciting experience, so enjoy the journey and always put yourself first.

Making Friends

Friendship is one of the most important aspects of our social lives. So, what makes a healthy friendship tick? Healthy friendships are built on trust, respect, and mutual support. You know you've got a good friend when they're there for you through thick and thin, cheering you on during the highs and offering a shoulder to lean on during the lows.

Now, when it comes to meeting new people and forming friendships, it's all about putting yourself out there. Join clubs or extracurricular activities that align with your interests, strike up conversations with classmates or teammates, or attend social events in your community. Remember, making friends is all about finding common ground and shared interests, so don't be afraid to be yourself and let your personality shine.

But, sometimes friendships run their course, or you realize that a relationship is more toxic than supportive. You know what? It's alright. Terminating a toxic friendship is always challenging, but it's crucial to prioritize your well-being. Be honest and respectful with your friend about your feelings, and give yourself permission to walk away from relationships that no longer serve you positively. Remember, it's not about burning bridges but recognizing when it's time to let go and move on to healthier connections.

Peer and Social Pressure

We've all been there—faced with situations where our friends or peers might want us to do something that we're not entirely comfortable with. It could be anything from skipping class to trying drugs or alcohol. But here's the thing: It's okay to say no. In fact, it's more than OK—it's crucial to stand up for what you believe in and make decisions that align with your values and goals rather than letting other people call the shots for your life.

How can you withstand peer pressure and assert your autonomy in decision-making? Well, it starts with knowing yourself and what you stand for. Take some time to reflect on your values, interests, and goals, and don't be afraid to assert them when faced with peer pressure. Remember, true friends will respect your boundaries and support you in making decisions that are right for you.

Setting and upholding personal values is key to navigating social pressures. Whether it's sticking to your commitment to study, avoiding risky behaviors, or standing up for what you believe in, having a strong sense of personal values will guide you through tricky situations. And remember, it's okay to be different and go against the grain if it means staying true to yourself.

Lastly, don't be afraid to seek out friends who share your values and respect your boundaries. Surrounding yourself with like-minded individuals who support and uplift you can make all the difference when it comes to resisting peer pressure and staying true to yourself. So, stand tall, trust your instincts, and remember that you have the power to make choices that align with the person you want to be.

Building Supportive Networks

Having a supportive network of friends, mentors, and peers can be a game-changer in both your personal and professional lives. These are the people who have your back, offer guidance, and cheer you on through thick and thin. Whether you're facing challenges at school, navigating tough decisions, or pursuing your passions, having a strong support system can provide you with the encouragement and resources you need to thrive.

Now, let's discuss the value of teamwork and collaboration. Working together with others toward a common goal can lead to incredible outcomes. Whether you're collaborating on a group project, participating in team sports, or working on a community initiative, teamwork teaches you essential skills like communication, problem-solving, and compromise. Plus, it's a great way to learn from others, share ideas, and achieve things you couldn't accomplish alone.

And finally, let's talk about leadership. Leadership isn't just about being in charge--it's about inspiring others, guiding them toward a shared vision, and fostering a sense of unity and purpose. Whether you're leading a team project, organizing a volunteer effort, or serving as a mentor to others, leadership skills are essential for success in any endeavor. Plus, developing your leadership skills can help you become a more effective communicator, decision-maker, and problem-solver. All valuable qualities that will serve you well in all aspects of life.

Conflict Resolution

Conflict is a natural part of life. It happens when people have differing opinions, interests, or needs. Understanding the causes of conflict is the first step toward resolving it. It could stem from misunderstandings, competing priorities, or even personality clashes. By identifying the root cause of the conflict, you can better address the underlying issues and work toward a solution that satisfies everyone involved.

Now, let's move on to an effective resolution. One approach is active listening, where you genuinely hear and understand the other person's perspective without interrupting or judging. Another technique is finding common ground. Focusing on shared interests or goals can help bridge the gap between conflicting parties. Additionally, brainstorming solutions together and being open to compromise can lead to mutually beneficial outcomes.

However, perhaps the most important aspect of conflict resolution is empathy. Empathy is about putting yourself in the other person's shoes, understanding their feelings and experiences, and showing compassion. By embracing empathy during conflicts, you increase the chances of discovering mutual understanding and achieving a resolution that honors the needs and emotions of all parties involved.

For example, let's say you and your friend disagree about which movie to watch. Instead of arguing or insisting on your choice, you could practice active listening to understand why your friend prefers a different movie. Then, you might suggest a compromise. Maybe you watch one movie this time and the other next time. By showing empathy and being willing to find a solution together, you can resolve the conflict without damaging your friendship.

So, remember, conflict is normal, but how you handle it makes all the difference.

Mentorship

Mentorship can be an absolute game-changer when it comes to your personal and professional growth.

A mentor is someone who can offer guidance, support, and valuable insights based on their own experiences. They can help you navigate challenges, set goals, and make important decisions.

So, how do you find a mentor? Start by identifying someone you admire and respect. Maybe it's a teacher, coach, family friend, or professional in your field of interest. Reach out to them, express your admiration, and ask if they'd be willing to mentor you. Remember, mentorship is a two-way street, so be respectful of their time and expertise and show gratitude for their support.

As you grow and learn, don't forget to pay it forward. Share your knowledge, skills, and experiences with others who may be seeking guidance. Whether it's offering advice to a younger student, volunteering in your community, or mentoring someone who's just starting out in your field, giving back not only helps others but also enriches your own life.

One of the most significant benefits of mentorship is the chance to gain insights from someone who has already traveled the road you're about to embark on. Mentors can offer practical advice, share lessons learned from their successes and failures, and provide encouragement during difficult times. This guidance can be invaluable as you navigate the ups and downs of life and work towards achieving your goals.

ACTIVITY: Reflection and Growth

Take some time to reflect on your social interactions over the past week. Write down an instance where you felt your social skills were particularly effective and helped you navigate a situation successfully. Then, jot down an instance where you thought you could have handled a social interaction better and consider how you might approach similar situations differently in the future. Finally, identify one new social skill you'd like to work on developing and brainstorm some actionable steps you can take to improve in that area. It could be anything from setting healthy boundaries to conflict resolution or assertiveness.

Chapter 11
Safety Skills

By failing to prepare, you are preparing to fail.
—Benjamin Franklin

In a world full of uncertainties, one of the most empowering things you can do as a teen is to master the art of safety and preparedness. This chapter delves into the crucial life skills that help you anticipate potential challenges and effectively mitigate risks. From personal safety tips to emergency preparedness, we'll explore strategies to keep you confident and secure in various situations.

Online Security

You've heard the terms "hackers" and "online scams" thrown around, right? But what do they really mean for you? Well, it means that there are bad people out there who wish to harm or steal from you. Yeah—that's the honest truth. It's up to you to keep your personal info safe while you're surfing the web, gaming, or just hanging out online. The good news is that there are some simple skills you can use to stay safe.

Let's break it down: First, your passwords are like the keys to your digital kingdom. Make them strong and unique for each account—mix up letters, numbers, and symbols to create a fortress that's tough to crack. Using the same password everywhere? It's not cool because if one site gets hacked, all your accounts could be at risk.

Next up, be super skeptical about emails or messages that seem off. You know the type—strange links, promises of free stuff, or someone claiming to need your help transferring money. These are classic bait for scams. If something feels weird, trust your gut and don't click.

When it comes to your personal details, think before you share. Social media can seem like fun and games until someone uses your info in ways you never intended. That awesome vacation pic or your phone number might seem harmless to post. Still, they can actually make you a target for identity theft or even online bullies. Ask yourself: "Who really needs to see this?" before you hit share.

And remember, knowledge is like your secret weapon when it comes to tech safety. Get to know the tools and apps you use. Check out their security settings and use them. Not sure about something or feeling uneasy about a message or an online interaction? Reach out for help. Talk to someone you trust, like a parent or a teacher, or look up reliable tech advice online.

Staying safe online isn't just about dodging hackers—it's about making smart choices and knowing how to protect yourself in the digital world. Stay curious, stay cautious, and keep your digital life locked down tight!

Roadside Emergencies

Roadside emergencies can be unpredictable, ranging from minor mechanical issues to major accidents. Imagine you're driving, and suddenly your engine starts making a strange noise, steam begins billowing from under the hood, or worse, you're involved in a collision. In any roadside emergency, knowing how to react swiftly and safely is crucial.

When trouble strikes, the first step is *always to prioritize safety*. If it's possible and safe to do so, guide your vehicle to the side of the road, well away from moving traffic. Turn on your hazard lights immediately to signal to other drivers that you need assistance, and they should proceed with caution around you.

Once you're safely parked, assess what's happening. If you see smoke or steam from the engine compartment, it could indicate an overheating problem or a fluid leak—do not attempt to open the hood until the engine has cooled, as this could cause injuries. If there's a strange noise coming from the engine, it could suggest a serious mechanical failure that might need professional attention.

In scenarios where you're involved in an accident, check for any injuries to yourself or passengers first. If medical attention is needed, call 911 right away.

Even in minor collisions where everyone seems fine, it's wise to contact the police to file a report for insurance purposes.

If the situation is beyond your ability to fix, like engine failure or significant vehicle damage, calling for roadside assistance is a sensible next step. They can provide towing, technical support, or even just more robust tools to help manage the situation.

Remember, the key to handling any roadside emergency effectively is to stay calm. Panic can cloud judgment and lead to poor decisions. By staying composed, you'll be able to think more clearly, evaluate the situation better, and decide the best course of action. Whether you end up needing to fix a minor issue yourself or require professional help, knowing you have a plan and can remain calm will make all the difference.

Learn to Swim

Swimming isn't just about having a good time in the water; it's a valuable skill that can keep you safe in any aquatic environment. Whether you're chilling at the beach, splashing around in a pool, or even out on a lake adventure, knowing how to swim means you're equipped to handle yourself in the water, reducing the risk of accidents and giving you the freedom to fully enjoy water-based activities.

Now, when it comes to learning how to swim, we're talking about more than just doggy paddling or doing cannonballs. It takes mastering fundamental skills like floating effortlessly, treading water like a pro, and getting comfortable with basic strokes like freestyle and backstroke. Once you've got these down, you'll be ready to tackle more advanced techniques like breaststroke and butterfly or even try your hand at cool water sports like surfing or diving.

But here's the thing—learning to swim isn't a one-and-done deal. It's a skill that you can keep honing and refining throughout your life. That means considering things like taking swimming lessons to brush up on your technique or joining a swim team to push yourself and improve your endurance. And, of course, regular practice is key to maintaining your skills and feeling confident in any water scenario.

So, whether you're a newbie or a seasoned swimmer, there's always something new to learn and explore in the world of swimming!

Extinguish A Fire

So, you find yourself staring down a fire. Your heart's racing, time is doing that weird slow-mo thing, and suddenly you're the lead in an action movie—except this isn't Hollywood, it's your kitchen.

Knowing how to deal with a fire isn't just for the pros; it's crucial for any teen who might need to step up as the hero in their own home drama. Here's your quick guide to handling those flames, whether it's time to bust out a fire extinguisher, smother the fire, or grab the phone for a potentially life-saving chat with 911.

We're going deep on this one because knowing this stuff can potentially make the difference between a little stove-top fire and your house being burnt to the ground. Stay sharp, stay safe, and let's keep things cool (literally) when things start heating up. Let's get into it.

Recognizing the Type of Fire

Before you act, it's crucial to identify what kind of fire you're dealing with. Fires involving everyday materials like wood and paper require different handling than those fueled by grease or electrical issues. Knowing the source can dictate whether to use a fire extinguisher or another method to douse the flames.

Smothering the Flame

If a fire breaks out from a small source, like a pan on the stove, smothering the flames might be your best bet, especially if you don't have an extinguisher handy.

1. Cover the Flames: For a pan fire, use a metal lid or a cookie sheet to cover the pan completely. This cuts off the oxygen and smothers the flames. Do not use glass, as it can shatter from the heat.

2. Turn Off the Heat: Once covered, turn off the burner. Do not move the pan; let it cool completely to avoid reigniting the fire.

3. Avoid Water: Never throw water on a grease fire. It can cause the oil to splash and spread the flames even more dangerously.

Using a Fire Extinguisher

1. Select the Correct Extinguisher: Ensure you have the correct type of extinguisher. A multi-purpose extinguisher labeled "ABC" is suitable for most fires you'll encounter at home.

2. PASS Technique: Once you have the proper extinguisher, remember the PASS technique:

• **Pull:** Pull the pin to break the tamper seal.

• **Aim:** Aim low, pointing the extinguisher nozzle at the base of the fire.

• **Squeeze:** Squeeze the handle to release the extinguishing agent.

• **Sweep:** Sweep the nozzle from side to side, covering the area of the fire until it's completely out.

Using an extinguisher can be effective, but it requires calm and precision. Practice this technique in advance so you're ready if the need arises.

When to Call 911

Sometimes, the best action is to retreat and call for help. Here are scenarios when you should dial 911:

1. The Fire Grows: If the fire is getting out of control control, it's time to call 911.

2. No Extinguisher Available: If you don't have access to a fire extinguisher or the fire is not smotherable, get out and call for help.

3. Smoke Becomes Excessive: Too much smoke can be hazardous to breathe. If you see heavy smoke, it's safer to leave the area and let professionals handle the situation.

Preventative Measures

Prevention is your best defense against fires:

• Regularly check smoke detectors and replace batteries as needed.

• Keep flammable materials away from stoves and heaters.

• Never leave candles unattended.

Learning how to put out fires is not just about saving your stuff—it's about potentially saving lives, maybe even your own. Getting the skills necessary for dealing with flames means you're ready for action if things get fiery. Stay cool under pressure, make smart moves, and don't forget—sometimes the hero move is to call 911 and get out. Remember, safety first, heroics second!

First Aid Skills

Picture this: you're chilling with your friends, having a grand old time, when suddenly, someone takes a spill and scrapes their knee. It may seem minor, but knowing how to handle the situation calmly and quickly can make all the difference.

First things first: PANIC!!!

Only kidding, c'mon!

Seriously, in these moments, it's easy to get caught up in the moment and add unnecessary stress to the situation. Take a deep breath and *calmly* spring into action!

Grab your trusty first aid kit and assess the situation. Is it a minor scrape that just needs a little TLC, or is it something more serious that might require a trip to the doctor? In technical terms, if it's what one would call a "boo-boo", then break out the antiseptic wipes and get to work.

Clean the wound gently but thoroughly, making sure to get rid of any dirt or debris. Then, apply some antibiotic ointment to help prevent infection and speed up healing.

Finally, cover the wound with a bandage or gauze, depending on its size (and your friend's preference for cartoon characters or superheroes). Give your friend a pat on the back for being such a trooper, and then get back to your regularly scheduled fun!

See? With a bit of know-how and a dash of humor, you can handle any minor first-aid situation. Just remember, if it's something more serious, don't hesitate to call for help.

But what about being prepared for emergencies on the go? That's where a simple first aid kit comes in handy. You don't need anything fancy.

Here are the 10 basic components of a simple first-aid kit:

- Bandages
- Antiseptic wipes
- Antibiotic ointment
- Gauze pads

- Medical tape
- Scissors
- Tweezers
- Instant cold pack
- Instant hot pack
- Disposable gloves

Keep your kit in a readily accessible spot, whether it's in your backpack, car, or even your bedroom, so you can grab it quickly when needed. And don't forget to check and replenish your supplies regularly to ensure everything's up-to-date and ready for action.

Disaster Preparedness

When the skies darken and the winds howl, the world can go from mundane to menacing in a heartbeat. Whether it's a fierce hurricane, an earth-shaking quake, or a tornado that threatens to send everything flying, being prepared isn't just wise—it's essential. Here's how you can stand strong and stay smart when nature decides to go off-script.

Know Your Enemies

First of all, understand the types of disasters most likely to visit your area. Hurricanes? Tornadoes? Earthquakes? Each villain has its own playbook, so your battle plan will depend on who's most likely to knock on your door. Get to know these forces of nature—what triggers them, how they behave, and how to tell when they're about to crash your party.

Emergency Kits: Your Disaster Day Pack

Think of your emergency kit like your go-to-the-beach bag—except instead of snacks and sunblock, this one's stocked with survival essentials. Here's your packing list:

• **Water:** One gallon per person per day for at least three days.

• **Food:** A stash of non-perishable items that could last you through a weekend music fest.

• **Lights and Power:** Flashlights, extra batteries, maybe a solar-powered charger if you want to stay really connected.

• **First Aid Kit:** Because sometimes the party gets rough, and you need to patch up a friend—or yourself.

• **Personal Documents:** Keep copies of key documents like your ID and insurance. Digital copies in a waterproof case can be a game-changer.

• **Extra Clothes and Blankets:** Because weather doesn't always follow the forecast, staying warm and dry isn't just comfortable; it's potentially life-saving.

Make a Plan

Choreograph your moves before the chaos starts. Where will you meet your family if your house becomes the next blockbuster disaster scene? How will you get in touch if cell towers decide to take a day off? Plan your escape routes, designate a meeting spot, and have a backup for your backup.

Stay Informed

Keep an ear to the ground—or, more accurately, an eye on your phone. Apps and alerts from reliable sources like the National Weather Service can give you the heads-up you need to either buckle down or bounce before things get hairy. Knowledge is power, and in this case, it's also safety.

Practice Makes Prepared

Run drills like they're dress rehearsals. The more you practice, the less likely you'll freeze if the big show happens when you least expect it. Earthquake drills, tornado drills, or even just a fire drill at home can make the difference between panic and poise.

Community Connections

Connect with your community for larger disasters. Neighbors looking out for neighbors can create a network of helpers because sometimes, the cavalry you're waiting for is just next door.

With your emergency kit packed, your strategies set, and your drills dialed in, you're not just sitting tight for the storm to clear—you're well-prepared to handle whatever comes your way safely and confidently.

ACTIVITY: Disaster Preparedness Kit

Building a simple disaster preparedness kit is easy and essential, especially for people who live in areas prone to natural disasters such as hurricanes, earthquakes, or tornados.

Start by picking a sturdy backpack or bin to store your items. Pack a bottle of water and some non-perishable snacks like granola bars or dried fruits. Include a flashlight with extra batteries and a first aid kit with basic supplies such as band-aids and antiseptic wipes. Don't forget a change of clothes and sturdy shoes suitable for your climate. Add personal items like a toothbrush, toothpaste, and any medications you might need. It's also smart to have copies of important documents like your ID in a waterproof bag. Lastly, throw in a few small bills for cash and a book or game to keep you occupied.

Store your kit in an easy-to-reach place so you can grab it quickly in an emergency. This kit will help you stay prepared and safe if a disaster strikes.

Chapter 12

Household Skills

Everyday acts within the home are more powerful than you might think. –Rod Dreher

In this chapter, we'll explore the essential tasks and responsibilities that keep a home running smoothly. From chores to basic maintenance, mastering these skills not only improves the functionality of your living space but also fosters independence and self-sufficiency.

We'll explore various aspects of household management, providing practical tips and strategies to confidently tackle common tasks.

Make Your Space Ship Shape

Having a well-organized space is a personal haven where you can think clearly and feel at ease. Keeping things tidy can seriously boost your mood and productivity, whether it's your bedroom, study area, or even your digital spaces.

Here's how to get things ship shape:

1. Start with a Clean Sweep: Begin by decluttering. Take everything off your desk, out of your drawers, and off your floor. Sort through it all. Do you really need six different blue pens or that t-shirt from a 5th-grade field trip? It might be time to say goodbye if it doesn't serve a purpose or bring you joy.

2. Designate Spaces: Once you've whittled down your possessions, decide where everything should go. Assign specific spots for your books, clothes, gadgets, and everything else. This way, you'll know exactly where to find things when needed and where to put them back after using them.

3. Get Storage-Smart: Utilize boxes, baskets, and organizers to keep your things tidy. Clear storage containers are great because you can see what's inside without digging through them. Use drawer dividers for smaller items like socks or stationery to avoid becoming a jumbled mess.

4. Keep a Routine: Make tidying a regular part of your routine. Spend a few minutes each day putting things back in their places. This will prevent clutter from building up and keep your space looking neat without needing major clean-up sessions.

5. Personalize Your Organization: Make your space yours. If you're into tech, set up a charging station for all your devices. If you're a fashion enthusiast, organize your closet in a way that makes it easy to pick your outfits. Are you a musician, photographer, or skateboarder? Your space should reflect your interests and make them easier to manage.

6. Digital Clean-Up: Don't forget about your digital spaces. Organize your study files into folders, keep your desktop clutter-free, and unsubscribe from emails you never read. A tidy digital space can enhance your focus just as much as a physical one.

7. Regular Reassessments: Every once in a while, take a step back and assess your space. As your interests and activities change, so might your organizational needs. Reevaluate what's working and what's not, and make adjustments to keep your space functional and refreshing.

Creating and maintaining an organized space can transform it from a chaos zone into your personal command center. It's not just about cleanliness; it's about crafting an environment where you can flourish. So take charge, get organized, and enjoy the calm and focus that comes with a well-laid-out space.

Laundry Basics

Unless you're a big fan of pink T-shirts, you should keep those red socks away from your white clothes. Separate your laundry into piles—whites, darks, and colors. Easy-peasy.

Check those clothing labels to see if they're machine washable and what temperature they can handle. Nobody wants their favorite shirt shrinking in the wash! Use the appropriate detergent and set your machine to the appropriate cycle. And remember, cold water is usually best for preserving colors and preventing shrinking.

When it comes to drying, air drying is your friend for delicate items like sweaters or jeans that you want to keep looking fresh. But for things like towels and sheets, the dryer works like a charm. Just toss in a dryer sheet to keep things smelling nice and static-free.

Last but not least, folding. Trust me, a little folding goes a long way in keeping your clothes looking neat and tidy. Take your time, fold along the seams, and voilà! Your clothes are ready to go back in the drawers or closet, all nice and organized. And hey, if you need a little extra help, there's no shame in watching a YouTube tutorial or two.

Surface Cleaning

Keeping your space clean is more than a chore; it's about crafting a sanctuary where you can unwind, focus, and have fun. Let's explore the key cleaning tasks that can transform your room, apartment, or home into a refreshing retreat.

Begin by sweeping. Grab a broom and clear away any dirt or debris on hard flooring surfaces like tile or wood. This is your initial move to prepare the area for a more thorough cleaning. After you've swept up the larger particles, it's time to switch to vacuuming. Vacuuming is essential for removing finer dust and particles embedded in carpet fibers or hidden in corners. Be sure to vacuum those tricky spots under the bed and behind furniture where dirt tends to accumulate.

Next up, dusting. Armed with a duster or a simple microfiber cloth, go over all surfaces. Begin with higher items like shelves and work your way down to tables and chair legs. Remember, dust can be sneaky, so keep an eye out for less obvious places like the tops of doors and picture frames.

When it comes to wiping surfaces, an all-purpose cleaner is your best friend. Spray and wipe down everything from countertops to desks, not forgetting light switches and door handles, which can collect germs.

I saved the best for last...

Next, let's dive into the glamour of bathroom cleaning! Arm yourself with a trusty scrub brush and your bravest smile—it's time to battle the germs in their natural habitat. Tackle the toilet with the enthusiasm of a knight in shining armor, conquer the tub like a pirate seizing a ship, and polish that sink until it sparkles like your personality. Armed with your disinfectant of choice, leave behind a trail of fresh scents and slain germs.

Clothing Maintenance

Nobody likes wrinkly clothes, right? Grab your iron, set it to the appropriate heat setting for your fabric, and start smoothing out those wrinkles. Just focus on button-down shirts, dresses, slacks, etc. No need to iron your undies, but hey—if you prefer knowing that underneath it all you're sporting crisp, wrinkle-free bloomers, then by all means, knock yourself out.

Next, stains. Whether it's spaghetti sauce or grass stains from your latest soccer game, stains happen. But fear not! With a bit of know-how, you can banish those stains like a pro. Treat stains promptly with a stain remover or a bit of dish soap before tossing them in the wash. And don't forget to check the care label first to ensure you're using the correct method for your fabric.

Ah, the noble art of button reattachment—a rite of passage for every teen! It's simple: grab a needle and choose your thread, ideally in a shade that doesn't scream, "*I did this myself in semi-darkness.*" Secure that rogue button while taking care not to perforate your paw. Not only re-attaching a button save your favorite shirt from an untimely farewell, but you'll also feel like a DIY superhero. Who knew such a tiny task could boost your street cred in the world of practical life skills?

Packing a Suitcase

Nothing to it, right? Toss in 2 heaping arm-fulls of random clothes from the floor - far too much for the lid to close without a liberal application of brute force—place your full body weight on the lid like a human pancake to just baaaaarely get the latch to catch—and VOILA...

A *"packed"* suitcase.

That's one way to do it, but here's another:

Jot down all the essentials you'll need based on where you're going, how long you'll be there, and what the weather will be like. This way, you won't forget anything important.

Instead of folding your clothes, try rolling them up. This saves a ton of space and helps prevent wrinkles, too. You can also stuff smaller items, like socks and underwear, inside your shoes to maximize space.

While you're packing your suitcase, think about what you'll need easy access to during your trip. Stuff like chargers, toiletries, and any important documents should go in a separate compartment or on top so you can grab them quickly.

And don't forget about being prepared for anything! Pack a small first-aid kit with essentials like Band-Aids, lip balm, and allergy medicine, just in case. Oh, and always remember to leave a little extra room in your suitcase for any souvenirs you might pick up along the way.

Saving on Utilities

Little changes can add up to big savings over time. So, remember to turn off lights when you leave a room, unplug electronics when you're not using them, and try to use natural light during the day instead of turning on lamps.

Now, when it comes to your appliances, there are a few things you can do to be more efficient. For starters, make sure your fridge and freezer are set to the right temperature—not too cold, not too warm. Also, try to run your dishwasher and washing machine with full loads to make the most of each cycle. And if you've got air conditioning, consider setting it a few degrees warmer in the summer and using fans to help circulate the cool air.

These might seem like small changes, but they can really add up when it comes to saving on your utility bills. Plus, it's good for the environment too!

Yardwork

Taking care of your yard might not sound like the most exciting task, so I'll do my best to spice things up a bit...

- Depending on your local climate and the mood of your grass, you might need to mow every week to keep your lawn from turning into a suburban jungle. Make sure to adjust your lawnmower height based on the type of grass you have and the time of year.
- Grab those hedge clippers and style those bushes like you're the barber of the burbs. Overgrown bushes can make your yard look messy, so grab some hedge trimmers and give them a good trim to keep them in shape.
- Now, for the delightful task of weeding. These sneaky green intruders can overrun your yard faster than teens raiding the fridge after school. Arm yourself with a weeding tool, or go old school and yank those weeds with your hands—just pretend you're pulling out the vegetables you don't like from your dinner plate.
- The finishing touch: yard cleanup! Sticks, debris, and those leaves from last autumn that thought they could stay forever? Time to break out the leaf blower and go full hurricane on that mess. Aim to make your yard so

pristine that it could feature on the cover of "Impeccable Lawns Monthly" or at least win a nod of approval from nosy neighbors.

Basic House Maintenance

Getting the hang of some basic DIY home repair skills can be a total game-changer. You know, the little things—like sorting out a leaky tap, unblocking the sink, or even patching up the elbow-shaped hole in your bedroom wall after that epic Nerf battle went south. Handling these repairs on your own can be quite empowering and often more straightforward than you might think.

It's important to have a basic toolkit. Essentials like a hammer, screwdriver set, adjustable wrench, pliers, and a tape measure can make a big difference. With these tools in hand, you're ready to tackle most of the common household issues that might pop up.

Don't forget to use YouTube as a resource. It's filled with how-to videos that can guide you through almost any household repair. Just search for what you need, like "how to fix a leaky tap" or "how to patch drywall," and you'll find detailed tutorials that can help you step-by-step. It's a great way to build your skills and confidence.

However, know your limits. For repairs that involve electricity, gas, or anything that feels beyond your skill level, it's safer to call in a professional. Also, if you attempt a repair and it doesn't go as planned, don't hesitate to seek help. Sometimes, it's wiser to call in an expert rather than risk making a problem worse.

Owning a Pet

Now, having a pet can be super rewarding, but it's also a big responsibility. First off, there's the daily stuff like feeding, exercising, and grooming. You've got to make sure your pet stays healthy and happy, just like you would for yourself.

But, hey, it's not all work and no play! Pets bring tons of joy and companionship into your life. They're always there to cuddle up with or play fetch when you need a break from studying. Plus, having a pet can even boost your mood and reduce stress. It's like having a built-in best friend!

Now, here's the real talk. Pets aren't just a short-term commitment—they're in it for the long haul. You'll need to plan for their care and well-being for years to come. That means regular vet check-ups, vaccinations, and maybe even unexpected medical bills. And let's not forget about the cost of food, toys, and other supplies.

So, before you bring home that adorable ball of fur, or feathers, or scales, or... whatever a hedgehog has—make sure you're ready for the responsibility and the financial commitment that comes with it.

Recycling

Recycling is a vital practice that transforms used materials like paper, plastic, glass, and metal back into valuable resources, thereby conserving natural materials and reducing environmental strain.

To truly make a difference with recycling, it's crucial to properly sort your recyclables, ensuring they are placed in the appropriate bins as determined by your local waste management guidelines. Effective sorting maximizes the potential for these materials to be processed and repurposed, playing a significant role in promoting sustainability.

By adopting and advocating for diligent recycling habits, you help sustain an ongoing cycle of reuse that benefits both the environment and society. This proactive approach not only aids in reducing landfill waste but also lessens the greenhouse gas emissions that come from manufacturing new products.

Engaging in recycling is a straightforward yet impactful way to contribute to environmental conservation and encourage a culture of sustainability among your peers and within your community.

Composting

Composting is a highly effective eco-practice that benefits both the environment and your garden. It involves the natural breakdown of organic materials such as fruit and vegetable scraps, eggshells, coffee grounds, and yard waste like leaves and grass clippings. By collecting these items in a compost bin or simply heaping them in a designated spot in your yard, you set the stage for nature to do its work. Over time, these organic materials decompose and transform into a nutrient-rich soil additive.

This natural process results in a potent compost that acts as an organic fertilizer, enriching the soil and promoting robust plant growth without the use of chemical fertilizers. Engaging in composting not only reduces the amount of waste that ends up in landfills but also returns valuable nutrients to the soil, enhancing its quality and fertility.

Once your compost is ready, it can be used in a variety of ways to boost the health and vitality of your garden. You can mix it into garden beds to improve soil structure and nutrient content, use it as a top dressing for lawns and flower beds, or incorporate it into potting mixes for container gardening. The rich, organic material helps retain moisture in the soil, supports root development, and fosters overall plant health.

Starting a composting routine is a straightforward way to contribute positively to environmental sustainability. It's rewarding to see everyday waste repurposed into something that can dramatically improve the soil of your garden. Composting is a smart, sustainable choice that benefits the planet and helps you cultivate a greener, more vibrant garden.

ACTIVITY: Create a Household Chore Chart

Creating a household chore chart is a practical way to ensure everyone contributes to maintaining the home. Here's how you can make this activity manageable and even enjoyable:

1. Gather The Fam: Bring all family members together for a meeting. This ensures everyone has a say and understands their responsibilities.

2. List Tasks: Write down all the chores that need to be done regularly, such as laundry, dishes, vacuuming, and taking out the trash. Don't forget less frequent tasks like cleaning windows or organizing the garage.

3. Assign Chores: Divide the chores among family members according to their abilities and schedules. Be fair and considerate—some tasks may be easier for some than others.

4. Schedule Days: Assign specific days for each chore. This could be daily, like dishes, or weekly, like vacuuming. Having a set schedule helps prevent any confusion about who needs to do what and when.

5. Create the Chart: Use a large poster board or a digital app if everyone is tech-savvy. Mark the chart with colorful markers, stickers, or digital icons to make it visually appealing and easy to read.

6. Decorate and Display: Let everyone decorate the chart with markers, stickers, or drawings. This makes the process fun and gives the chart a personal touch. Then, place it in a common area where it's easily visible to all family members.

7. Review and Adjust: After a few weeks, review the chart together. This is a good time to make any necessary adjustments based on what's working or not. This can keep the system fair and flexible.

Household Skills

A chore chart isn't just a way to keep your home tidy; it's also a tool for learning responsibility and boosting teamwork. It's about more than just chores—it's about working together to make your home a better place for everyone.

Chapter 13
Health and Well-Being Skills

Your body is your most priceless possession; take care of it. –Jack Lalanne

We're about to begin a journey that's all about feeling fantastic inside and out. From fueling your body with the right foods to finding ways to relax and recover, I've got you covered. So, let's get right into it and explore how you can live your best, healthiest life.

Breaking Bad Habits

First up, let's unpack something quite surprising: about 40% of what you do every day isn't the result of active choices but habits—those little routines you hardly think about (Lindner, 2023b). This means a big chunk of your life runs on autopilot. So, it's super important to hone in on ditching those not-so-great habits that might be dragging you down. You know the ones I'm talking about—staying up way too late, caught up in endless social media feeds, or constantly reaching for a bag of chips instead of an apple or some carrots.

Initially, these habits might not seem like a big deal. What's a little late-night scrolling or a few extra chips, right? But here's the kicker: over time, these small choices accumulate, gradually taking a toll on both your physical and mental health. That's why recognizing these habits is the first crucial step.

The next step? Actively replacing them with positive ones. Instead of mindless scrolling, why not try winding down with a book or planning your next day to boost productivity? Swap out junk food for healthier snacks that leave you feeling energized rather than sluggish.

Breaking habits doesn't just mean stopping something; it's about transforming your routine to support a healthier, happier you. It's like upgrading your system software—you're enhancing how you operate on a daily basis, which can lead to significant improvements in how you feel and perform.

So, take the reins on those 40% of your actions that are habitual. Make them count for something good, and you'll start to see just how much better life can be when you're in control of your habits rather than them controlling you.

Establishing Healthy Habits

Have you heard of habit stacking? This clever technique, which involves linking a new habit to an existing one, can significantly boost your chances of making the new habit stick (Seaver, 2024).

For instance, if you're looking to start journaling every day, consider doing it right after your morning cup of tea or just before you hit the hay at night. By anchoring this new activity to a part of your routine that's already well-established, you effectively make the new habit part of your daily flow without much extra effort.

It's important to note that when trying to build new habits, you'll inevitably encounter setbacks. They're a natural part of trying to change or introduce new habits—no one gets it right all the time! The important thing isn't to dwell on the slip-ups or get down on yourself. Instead, see each setback as an opportunity to learn and refine your approach.

Maybe your timing needs tweaking, or perhaps your goals need to be a bit more attainable. Whatever adjustments you need to make, remember that setbacks are not roadblocks but merely bumps along the path.

Keep your spirits up and your focus forward. With persistence and a bit of strategic planning, these new healthy habits will soon weave seamlessly into the fabric of your daily life, becoming as natural and unconscious as any of your old habits. Before you know it, you'll be living a healthier, more intentional life with ease.

Sleep

You might think that sleep is just something you do at the end of the day to recharge, but it's so much more than that. Getting enough sleep is crucial for your physical health, mental well-being, and overall performance in everything you do.

Here's a little tidbit that might make you think twice about skimping on your sleep: people who clock in less than six hours of shut-eye each night are up to four times more likely to catch a cold than those who get a solid seven hours or more. Crazy, huh?

It turns out that skimping on sleep can really affect your immune system, not to mention your overall health. And when your health isn't up to snuff, your performance—whether at school, work, or in life—takes a hit, too. Moreover, when you're running low on sleep, it's not just your body that suffers.

Research shows that being sleep-deprived can mess with the mind to a similar level as someone who is intoxicated. Yeah, this is serious stuff! So, if you want to keep on top of your game, both mentally and physically, making sure you get enough sleep is pretty crucial. It's not just about feeling rested; it's about keeping your performance on point.

So, how do you establish healthy sleep routines? Well, it starts with setting a consistent bedtime and wake-up time, even on weekends. This assists in regulating your body's internal clock, making it simpler to drift off to sleep and wake feeling rejuvenated.

Establishing a soothing bedtime ritual can also indicate to your body that it's time to relax. This might involve activities such as reading, enjoying a warm bath, or engaging in deep breathing exercises.

Here's something worth mentioning—if you struggle with insomnia, trouble falling asleep, or waking up throughout the night, there are some simple solutions that might help. For example, limiting screen time before bed can reduce the blue light exposure that can interfere with your sleep cycle. Cutting back on caffeine and heavy meals close to bedtime can also make it easier to drift off. And if you find yourself tossing and turning, try getting out of bed and doing something relaxing until you feel sleepy again.

Move It, Move It

It's no surprise that exercise is beneficial to our physical and mental health, but sometimes, it can be hard to get started. So, let's tackle those barriers together.

One significant barrier to exercise is a lack of time. Between school, homework, and hanging out with friends, it can feel like there's no time left for a workout. But here's the thing—you don't need hours in the gym to reap the benefits of exercise.

Even just 10 minutes a day of moderate activity can make a big difference. So, find activities you enjoy, whether it's dancing to your favorite tunes, going for a bike ride, or playing a pickup game of basketball with friends. The key is to make it fun!

Speaking of fun, there are a variety of exercise options out there. From cardio and strength training to yoga and dance, there's something for everyone. Don't be afraid to try new things keep it interesting. Who knows, you might discover a new passion along the way!

Now, let's address those sedentary activities that can sneak into our daily routines. Whether it's binge-watching Netflix, scrolling through social media for hours, or playing video games non-stop, these activities can take up a lot of our time and keep us glued to our seats. But remember every minute spent sitting is a missed opportunity to move your body and feel amazing. So, try to limit screen time and find ways to incorporate more activity into your day, like taking a walk during breaks or doing some stretches while watching TV.

Grooming and Hygiene

Grooming and hygiene: the unsung heroes of self-care. So, why is staying squeaky clean so crucial? Well, besides the obvious perks like not being the person everyone subtly scoots away from on the bus, good hygiene is your body's best defense against sneaky germs looking to throw a sick-day party. Plus, taking the time to scrub up and look sharp can boost your confidence. It's about feeling fabulous, staying healthy, and rocking that "*I definitely showered today*" glow.

So, what does a healthy grooming routine look like? It's all about finding what works for you and sticking to it. For example, make sure to brush your teeth at least twice a day and floss regularly to keep your smile bright and your mouth healthy. When it comes to bathing, aim to shower or bathe daily, especially after sweaty activities like sports or exercise. And don't forget to wash your hands frequently throughout the day to prevent the spread of germs—especially important during cold and flu season!

Everyone's routine will look a little different depending on their needs and preferences, but there are a few basics that everyone should have on hand. Things like deodorant to keep you smelling fresh, nail clippers to keep your nails neat and tidy, and toothpaste and a toothbrush to keep your smile sparkling. And let's not forget about skincare. A gentle cleanser, moisturizer, and sunscreen can go a long way in keeping your skin healthy and glowing.

Remember, taking care of yourself isn't just about looking good on the outside; you need to feel good on the inside, too. So, make sure to prioritize your grooming and hygiene routine as part of your overall self-care regimen.

Body Changes

This topic can be a bit like bringing up who put the empty milk carton back in the fridge—it's awkward, but someone's got to address it. Puberty, that wild ride every human signs up for without actually signing anything, is as normal as pineapple on pizza (a little controversial, but definitely a part of life). You grow taller seemingly overnight. Boys get muscles, girls get curves. Not to mention, hair starts auditioning for new roles all over your body. Yes, puberty is basically your body's own extreme makeover: teenage edition!

But every single one of these changes is entirely normal and nothing to be embarrassed about. We all go through it! Embracing your body's natural changes is an essential part of growing up and becoming comfortable in your own skin. Sure, it might feel a bit awkward at times, but remember that everyone around you is going through the same thing—even if they don't always show it.

In a world inundated with images of "ideal" bodies on social media and in magazines, it's common to feel inadequate. However, it's essential to understand that there's no such thing as a perfect body, and beauty manifests in various shapes, sizes, and forms.

Rather than fixating on outward appearance, it's beneficial to appreciate our bodies' *incredible capabilities*. Whether it's the ability to run, dance, or simply reading this book...

Think about it:

Your miracle of a body is able to understand the thoughts in MY HEAD by looking at thousands of little squiggly lines of ink on a sheet of paper. Isn't that just *insane*?

So, instead of worrying about whether you have the "right" body type, focus on keeping your body healthy and strong. Eat nutritious foods, get regular exercise, and make time for self-care activities that make you feel good about yourself from the inside out.

Skewed Media Reality

We all know that scrolling through Instagram or TikTok can be a lot of fun, but it's important to be aware of the impact that overexposure to social media can have on your well-being.

We've touched on this a little already, but one big thing to watch out for is the messages that social media sends us about what we should look like, how we should act, and what we should have. You've probably seen tons of posts showing people with perfect bodies, flawless skin, and seemingly perfect lives, right? It's *extraordinarily important* to remember that these images are seldom realistic.

Constant exposure to these kinds of images can make us feel like we're not good enough or like we're missing out on something. It can also lead to unhealthy comparisons with others and even feelings of anxiety or depression. That's why it's so important to be mindful of how much time you're spending on social media and to take breaks when you need to.

Now, I'm not saying that social media is all bad—far from it! It can be a great way to stay connected with friends, share fun moments, and even learn new things. The key is to cultivate healthy social media habits that prioritize your mental and emotional well-being.

So, how can you do that? Well, start by setting boundaries around your social media use. Maybe limit yourself to checking your accounts for a certain amount of time each day or take regular breaks from social media altogether. You can also curate your feed to include accounts that inspire and uplift you rather than ones that make you feel bad about yourself.

Remember, it's okay to unfollow accounts or take a break from social media if it's not making you feel good. Your mental health is far more important than likes or followers.

Substance Abuse Awareness

Even though teens should avoid being involved in such matters, it's crucial to acknowledge the possibility and know how to respond if needed.

Substance abuse refers to the harmful or excessive use of drugs or alcohol, and it can have severe consequences for your health, relationships, and future opportunities.

It's important to be aware of the signs of substance abuse, whether in yourself or others. These signs might manifest as changes in behavior, sudden shifts in mood, significant changes in weight, or neglecting usual responsibilities or interests. If you notice any of these signs in yourself or a friend, don't hesitate to seek help. Speaking up and reaching out for support is the first step toward getting the assistance necessary.

Living a substance-free life isn't just about saying no to drugs or alcohol—it's about making positive choices that support your health and well-being. Surround yourself with friends who share your values and support your decision to stay substance-free. Find healthy ways to cope with stress and pressure, like exercising, practicing mindfulness, or pursuing your passions.

It's also important to educate yourself about the dangers of substance abuse and how it can impact your life. Take the time to learn about the risks associated with different substances, and don't be afraid to ask questions or seek guidance from trusted adults.

Remember, you are in control of your choices and your future. By staying informed, seeking support when you need it, and making positive choices that align with your values, you can live a happy, healthy, and substance-free life.

Digital Detox

We all love scrolling through our feeds, checking out the latest memes, and staying connected with friends online. But have you ever stopped to think about how all that screen time might be affecting your mental health and real-life relationships?

It's like that moment when you realize you've been staring at your phone for so long that you've forgotten what the sky looks like. Spending too much time online can sometimes make us feel like we're not measuring up to the perfectly curated lives we see on our screens.

That's where the digital detox comes in. It's all about taking a break from social media and other digital distractions to give our minds a chance to reset and recharge (and maybe even remember what our friends look like in person). Whether it's for a few hours, a day, or even a whole week (gasp!), disconnecting from our devices can help us reconnect with ourselves and the people around us.

So, go ahead and unplug for a bit. Take a walk outside, hang out with friends in person, or pick up a hobby that doesn't involve screens, like knitting or extreme ironing (yeah—it's a thing).

Environmental Awareness

The environment we live in has a profound impact on our physical and mental health. Everything from the air we breathe to the food we consume plays a critical role in shaping our well-being.

Take air quality, for instance. Breathing in polluted air isn't just unpleasant—it can trigger a host of health issues, including asthma, allergies, and even more serious conditions like heart disease. This makes it clear why we each need to contribute to maintaining clean air.

How can we make a difference? Simple everyday actions can significantly reduce our environmental footprint. Opting to walk or bike instead of driving is a great start. It's not only good for the planet but also our health. Using energy-efficient appliances and reducing reliance on single-use plastics are other effective strategies. For instance, switching to a refillable water bottle instead of buying bottled water not only cuts down on plastic waste but also saves money in the long run.

By making these changes, we don't just improve our immediate surroundings, but we also contribute to a healthier planet. And a healthier planet means a healthier us. It's all interconnected, and every small action counts.

You Are What You Eat

Eating a diet packed with fresh fruits, vegetables, whole grains, and lean proteins does wonders for your health—it's not just about maintaining a healthy weight but also about enriching your body with essential nutrients.

When you choose foods that are grown locally and sustainably, you often get the added benefit of enhanced freshness. Such foods haven't been transported across vast distances, which usually means they retain more of their nutritional value by the time they reach your plate. This translates into more vitamins, minerals, and antioxidants in your diet—elements crucial for maintaining energy, boosting your immune system, and overall wellness.

But there's more to our daily consumption than just food; water plays an equally crucial role. Staying hydrated is essential for everything from cognitive function to digestion. Yet, access to clean drinking water is not a given for everyone. This makes it especially important for those of us who do have access to manage it responsibly.

Mindful practices like reducing shower times, promptly repairing leaks, and being careful not to overwater lawns can significantly minimize wastefulness. Such habits not only help preserve this vital resource but also contribute to a broader effort to ensure there's enough clean water available for all, promoting health and equity across communities.

ACTIVITY: Healthy Habit Tracker

Grab a piece of paper or use an app on your phone to create a simple chart with the days of the week listed horizontally and healthy habits listed vertically.

For example, you could include habits like drinking enough water, getting at least 30 minutes of exercise, eating a serving of fruits and veggies, getting enough sleep, and practicing self-care. Each day, check off or mark the habits you've completed.

At the end of the week, take a look at your tracker. Celebrate the habits you've consistently stuck to and reflect on any areas where you might want to improve. Maybe you notice that you're not getting enough sleep or that you could use a little more exercise. That's okay—use this insight to set goals for the upcoming week and keep working towards building healthier habits.

Remember, progress takes time, so be patient with yourself and celebrate every small victory along the way!

Chapter 14
Conclusion

Throughout this book, you've explored dozens of practical life skills that aren't taught in school but are crucial for navigating the journey into adulthood. By embracing and honing these skills, you're not just preparing for the future—*you're actively shaping it.*

So, as you step forward, do so with confidence, knowing that you possess the tools and knowledge to thrive in whatever challenges life may bring. And if one of those challenges happens to be folding a fitted sheet, well, just remember, *nobody actually knows how to do that one.*

As you close this book and prepare to set off on the next phase of your journey, remember that learning doesn't end here. Keep this book within reach, ready to revisit its pages whenever you encounter new challenges or need a refresher.

In closing, I want to leave you with this: **You are capable, resilient, and ready to face what challenges lie ahead.** With the life skills you've acquired, you have the tools to navigate the path to adulthood with confidence and grace. *You've got this.*

Believe in yourself, trust in your abilities, and embrace the journey with optimism. You hold the power to shape your future, and I firmly believe that you will do so with remarkable success.

Before we part ways, I have a single request to ask of you...

Chapter 15

Light The Beacon

You've reached the end of this book, and now you're armed with a wide variety of practical skills that will serve you well as you progress forward in life.

What's next?

It's time for you to help a person that you'll never meet.

You see, there are people out there who need this book—but they don't know where to find it.

By leaving a few thoughtful words in an Amazon review, you're doing more than just recommending a book; you're *lighting a beacon* that will show someone else how to gain the practical life skills they need.

Scan the QR code to light the beacon:

Light The Beacon

Thanks for allowing me to be a part of your journey! Your biggest fan,

~ Ben Clardy

Keep Going!

You're doing amazing, *so keep the momentum going!*

What do you feel like working on next?

Are you ready to start designing an achievable path toward your dream life or would you rather start fattening up your piggy bank?

To get you there, you've got:

Personal Finance For Teens: In this book, you'll learn many different ways to make money, how to save it, grow it, budget wisely, and start building financial independence. If you're ready to get a handle on your finances, this is the next book for you.

Growth Mindset For Teens: This one teaches you how to think the same way that star athletes, tech innovators, and high achievers do. If you'd like to drastically boost your confidence, create totally achievable goals, and start building your dream life, then this is your next book for you.

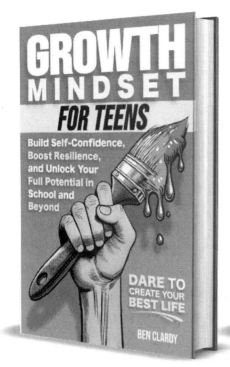

Just scan a QR code with your device's camera and you'll be whisked away to the page where you can grab your copy.

There's no wrong choice, and these books can be read in any order.

Congratulations for what you've accomplished thus far.

Here's to your bright future!

-Ben Clardy

Bibliography

Adams, R. (2024, January 23). Every year spent in school or university improves life expectancy, study says. *The Guardian*. https://www.theguardian.com/education/2024/jan/23/every-year-spent-in-school-or-university-improves-life-expectancy-study-says

Anthony, M. (2019). *Creative development in adolescents*. Scholastic.com. https://www.scholastic.com/parents/family-life/creativity-and-critical-thinking/development-milestones/creative-development-adolescents.html

Berger, R. (2014, April 30). *Top 100 money quotes of all time*. Forbes. https://www.forbes.com/sites/robertberger/2014/04/30/top-100-money-quotes-of-all-time/?sh=7f965c7e4998

Bird, L. (n.d.). *Larry Bird quotes*. Goodreads. https://www.goodreads.com/quotes/212675-a-winner-is-someone-who-recognizes-his-god-given-talents-works

Bourdain, A. (n.d.). *Anthony Bourdain quotes*. Goodreads. https://www.goodreads.com/quotes/676336-good-food-is-very-often-even-most-often-simple-food

Burg, B. (n.d.). *Bob Burg quotes*. Goodreads. https://www.goodreads.com/author/quotes/115311.Bob_Burg

Carnegie, D. (n.d.). *Dale Carnegie quotes*. Goodreads. https://www.goodreads.com/quotes/138569-when-dealing-with-people-remember-you-are-not-dealing-with

Chefalo, S. (2023, January 17). *The four pillars of emotional intelligence*. PACEsConnection. https://www.pacesconnection.com/blog/the-four-pillars-of-emotional-intelligence

Cousins, N. (n.d.). *Norman Cousins quotes*. Goodreads. https://www.goodreads.com/author/quotes/27594.Norman_Cousins

Danzie, J. (n.d.). *Jay Danzie quotes*. Goodreads. https://www.goodreads.com/quotes/792897-your-smile-is-your-logo-your-personality-is-your-business

Dreher, R. (n.d.). *Rod Dreher quotes*. Goodreads. https://www.goodreads.com/quotes/10662195-less-formal-everyday-acts-within-the-home-are-more-powerful

80 most inspiring emotional intelligence quotes (LEADERSHIP). (2023, February 27). Gracious Quotes. https://graciousquotes.com/emotional-intelligence/

Elsworthy, E. (2019, April 25). *These are the life skills teenagers lack, according to their parents*. The Independent. https://www.independent.co.uk/life-style/teenagers-life-skills-parents-children-survey-stress-budget-drive-a8886031.html

Fleming, W. (2022, June 20). *50+ awesome and inspirational quotes for teenagers*. Parenting Teens and Tweens. https://parentingteensandtweens.com/inspirational-quotes-for-teenagers/

Gallagher, A., & Gallagher, J. (n.d.). *Easy ultra creamy mac and cheese*. Inspired Taste. https://www.inspiredtaste.net/37626/easy-creamy-mac-and-cheese/

Gerten, K. (2022, June 20). *15 quotes on communicating with empathy*. Youth Dynamics. https://www.youthdynamics.org/15-quotes-on-communicating-with-empathy/

Jordan, M. (n.d.) *Michael Jordan quotes*. Goodreads. https://www.goodreads.com/quotes/38639-some-people-want-it-to-happen-some-wish-it-would

LaLane, J. (n.d.). *Jack LaLanne quotes*. QuoteFancy. https://quotefancy.com/quote/1283821/Jack-LaLanne-My-goal-has-always-been-to-help-people-help-themselves-Your-body-is-your

Lindenberg, B. (2022, September 22). *103+ critical thinking quotes that stimulate beautiful minds*. Food Truck Empire. https://foodtruckempire.com/jobs/critical-thinking-quotes/

Lindner, J. (2023a, December 8). *Communication facts and statistics [fresh research]*. Gitnux. https://gitnux.org/communication-facts-and-statistics/

Lindner, J. (2023b, December 20). *Habit statistics*. Gitnux. https://gitnux.org/habit-statistics/

Martha. (2014, August 25). *Hot fudge pudding cake*. A Family Feast®. https://www.afamilyfeast.com/hot-fudge-pudding-cake/

Bibliography

Martha. (2020, February 28). *Classic egg salad*. A Family Feast®. https://www.afamilyfeast.-com/classic-egg-salad/

National Organization for Women. (2019). *Get the facts*. National Organization for Women. https://now.org/now-foundation/love-your-body/love-your-body-whats-it-all-about/get-the-facts/

National Soft Skills Association. (2019, May 31). *The soft skills disconnect*. National Soft Skills Association. https://www.nationalsoftskills.org/the-soft-skills-disconnect/

1 in 5 U.S. teens lacks basic personal finance skills. (n.d.). National Endowment for Financial Education (NEFE). https://www.nefe.org/news/nefe-digest/2017/can-america-compete.aspx

Ramsey, D. (n.d.). *Dave Ramsey quotes*. Goodreads. https://www.goodreads.com/quotes/7752892-financial-peace-isn-t-the-acquisition-of-stuff-it-s-learning-to

Reid, S. (2024, February 5). *Gratitude: The benefits and how to practice it*. HelpGuide.org. https://www.helpguide.org/articles/mental-health/gratitude.htm

Robbins, T. (n. d.). *Tony Robbins quotes*. Goodreads. https://www.goodreads.com/quotes/877199-the-only-impossible-journey-is-the-one-you-never-begin

Scroggs, L. (2021). *Avoid the "urgency trap" with the Eisenhower matrix*. Todoist. https://todoist.-com/productivity-methods/eisenhower-matrix

Seaver, M. (2024, March 24). *Habit stacking makes new habits last—here's how it works*. Real Simple. https://www.realsimple.com/work-life/life-strategies/inspiration-motivation/habit-stacking

Swindoll, C. R. (2020). *Charles R. Swindoll quotes*. Goodreads. https://www.goodreads.com/au-thor/quotes/5139.Charles_R_Swindoll

Twain, M. (2020). *Mark Twain quotes*. Goodreads. https://www.goodreads.com/quotes/219455-the-secret-of-getting-ahead-is-getting-started-the-secret

Whiteside, E. (2022, September 17). *What is the 50/20/30 budget rule?* Investopedia. https://www.in-vestopedia.com/ask/answers/022916/what-502030-budget-rule.asp

Made in the USA
Las Vegas, NV
08 January 2025

0c956ab8-fa83-4e3f-9039-204122512bf6R01